Going Back… Forward

AF665031

Monisha Makhija

BookLeaf Publishing

Presentation by *BookLeaf Publishing*

Web: www.bookleafpub.com

E-mail: info@bookleafpub.com

ISBN: 9789360941840

First edition 2024

ACKNOWLEDGEMENTS

Although I've written this book, it wouldn't have been possible without the expert input of my daughter Sukriti Makhija, a journalist herself. Thank you, my Darling, for being so patient with me and for correcting me wherever I went wrong.

Karan Makhija – my son, who waited for me to finish writing a thought when he called.

My sister Mona Handa, for being with me through thick and thin.

Anuradha Matta and Namrita Singh, my besties, who listened to me carefully as I chalked out this idea for a book.

My well-wisher, who constantly insisted that I finish the book, and who painstakingly went through each word I wrote.

Siddhant Mathur who gave his valuable feedback as a scriptwriter.

Vishwas Makhija, who was the first one to support the idea of my writing, even when we were buried in work.

Above all, my parents Sunila and Pratap Khosla, my pillars of strength. I am what I am because of them.

CHAPTER 1

THE ARRIVAL AT THE GATE

The doors to Heaven were closed. The doors to Hell were closed.

Yamraj and Chitragupta were nowhere in sight. Something was wrong—other than the fact that I was dead.

The line at the entrance seemed out of place. Strangely, I had never heard of a line to get into Heaven or Hell. From what I remembered of my human life, once you pass, you are automatically taken to the door where your soul remains, until you are summoned to be born again.

"There is no place for us here," someone cried. They say that it is full!! Damn, the Corona Virus!!!!

It was 2020, and the world was at a standstill! The pandemic changed the way humans functioned. Meeting friends, going to work, and even grocery shopping seemed to be in the distant past. Now just the thought of being in the same room as your loved ones was full of doubts and sanitation procedures!

It ruined my life on earth, and now there wasn't any place in the afterworld as well. Bloody ridiculous!

Amongst the wails and cries, curses and prayers it was stifling. Maybe I was in Hell after all? But I couldn't see fires around me.

Stepping away from the crowd that had gathered, I reached into my sling for my cigarettes. Strange that I still had them. Weren't all worldly possessions left behind when you died? But I wasn't one to complain or ponder, at the risk of the cigarettes being whisked away as if I was still in school. I wandered about, trying to make some sense of the chaos. For sure I was at the helm of the 'other side.' All around me, I could see souls floating about, looking as confused as I was, no Yamraj to follow, no Chandragupta to count their sins, and not even St. Peter or Baba Nanak. Were we so corrupt a soul that the Gods had as well abandoned us to roam about?

I wouldn't be surprised, considering all that I had gone through in my life.

"Got a light on you? I forgot mine at home." The voice seemed vaguely familiar. "I swear if I have to stand here one more minute, I might just kill somebody."

"Dude they are all already as dead as you," I shot back. "Lighten up, it is not the end of the world."

Or was it? I still had no reason to believe that I was entirely and a hundred per cent dead. I mean, I hadn't been assigned a place in either world. And I had been out for a meeting, about five minutes ago. Maybe the doctors could perform a successful CPR on me.

"So, what happened to you?" I asked, trying hard to hold a conversation. "Let me guess, Corona?"

"Surprisingly, no." He paused for effect. "I was hale and hearty one minute, and walking home after a run. This moronic driver just came out of nowhere and blew me to death." The anger of a wasted life was quite evident in his voice.

I looked at him again, still trying to place him. He looked a bit familiar, and his voice was one that I had heard before, I was sure.

Horror dawned on me! No wonder the voice seemed familiar. Just a short time back, I was standing over him, and trying to understand his sputtering and hissing as he tried to breathe through a punctured lung and broken ribs.............

With a shaking breath, I whispered "I am so sorry." "Who did you leave behind?"

"My wife and kids," he sniffled. "And who did you leave behind and what happened to you?"

I did not have the nerves to tell him that his moronic driver was right in front of him! Although dead, he still oozed a lot of muscle strength, and I, in the sorry state of health that I was, still had the smoker's lungs and a middle-aged body.

"Covid-19", the lie slipped out easily. "And two grown-up kids, parents and an estranged husband."

"So, what do you think will happen to us now?" Extending him a cigarette and a lighter, I shrugged.

"None of this makes sense, who would have thought that you would need to stand in a line to let your fate be decided for you."

"I think we are about to find out what comes next," he said, pointing towards the gate.

CHAPTER 2

WHAT NEXT?

The throng of souls parted to make way for The Mighty Yamraj atop his bull. Chitragupta and St. Peter flanked him on both sides. It was a sight to behold. While alive, I had so many times dreamed of unity on earth but hadn't seen much. Us humans are forever fighting over religion, customs and traditions.

So much so that we have divided the Gods amongst us as well.

Here, at the threshold of the Other Side, seeing all the religious supremes, in discussion together, acted as a balm to my frazzled nerves.

“All right!!!! Listen up!!!!!”

By God, Yamraj’s voice was as loud as he was huge!!

"Sorry that you folks have no place to go to at this very moment," he said, "but we are now facing a crisis as well." "We do not have enough room for all of you, Heaven and Hell combined." Looking at the crowd with a sorry face, Yamraj continued, "We did not realise the magnitude of the Pandemic."

"Stop blaming God for everything"!!! He barked, looking at the sarcastic faces around him. "As if God would be so cruel. It was not an act of God that the Pandemic consumed the entire world...humans were to blame for this."

"We have come up with a solution which seems to be something that might work," Chitragupta took up the conversation.

"The Covid deaths, please step forward, on to the right, the old age onto the left. The rest of you remain where you are."

A flurry of movement caught me in a handful of people as compared to the huge crowd on the other side. About 50 odd in number.

The Covid corner was overflowing!!! Double damn the makers of the flu.

A hush fell over the group, as The Gates slowly opened up. Who would be going in?? Did I just attain Moksha??? Most likely not.
“We are breaking precedent this time," shouted St. Peter. The old age souls may please pass through The Gates. They go straight to Heaven. But remember, Chitragupta still has your records. So, when you come back to us after your next birth, we shall decide what needs to be done with you.”

“The Pandemics, please line up for a thorough check-up and cleansing. You obviously are not allowed anywhere until you are clean again. By the time this process finishes, we shall be able to accommodate you guys gradually, a few at a time.”

“The accidents/murders etc. Well! Well!! Well!!! We have a surprise in store for you clueless souls.”

Exchanging sly grins, and smirking at us, Yamraj said, “We are being very lenient towards you! I have decided to give you another chance.”

“YOU GET TO GO BACK TO YOUR LIVES.”

Wait! What! Did I just hear correctly, or was my hearing now impaired due to the accident that landed me here?? I looked around and saw my emotions mirrored in the small crowd around me.

"You can't be serious."

"What will we do if we go back?"

"Nobody will remember us any more!"

"We are dead to our loved ones; they have moved on."

Didn't time travel at a faster pace up here than on Earth?? What seemed like about an hour here, could easily have been 10 years on Earth. My children would have grown up, gotten married and had kids of their own now. My parents may or may not be alive. And my husband, well there is no telling what he would be up to now!!! I did not want to go back, did I??

One could see the indignation on every face, and Yamraj was in a fix. You could tell by the vein throbbing in his forehead. He looked at

Chitragupta pleadingly, asking him to help soothe the ruffled feathers of the ones who were going to be plunged back nevertheless.

"Come on people!!! We need you to cooperate with us. There is no place left in the Nether world anymore. Too many of you have died too soon." "This is not what we intended to happen."

"So, this was an act of God then!! Why blame just the Chinese for the pandemic, the Gods were involved as well."

"Are we so insignificant now? What about all the prayers and the *havans* we did, what about all our good deeds, what about just granting us moksha, and relieving us from this cycle?"

The accusations and questions kept flying around until Yamraj lost it finally.

"Quite"!! He thundered, red in the face and the pulse now clearly visible at the base of his neck and forehead.

"You talk about nirvana and moksha as if it is some sweet that we can hand out at will!!"

"Yes, you did your prayers and havan and good deeds, but your misdeeds weigh more!!"

"The Gods created you and your intelligence, but we did not tell you to hurt each other, or to develop biological warfare. The Gods were kind enough to give you a way out, by giving you prevention for the virus, but humans openly defied us, protests against wearing masks, and social distancing! Really? Are these your good deeds? Your prayers were answered, but you were too busy blaming each other to even pay attention to our intervention."

"This is all on you!!"

Controlling his angry outburst, Yamraj continued in a much calmer voice, "The aged have lived their lives, and quite frankly, we do care about the seniors unlike you all, so they go straight in."

"The Covid ones need a thorough procedure to get their soul ready for the next life. That would take a while for us even, too much has been damaged and gone bad, as per the standards on this side of the universe."

Giving us a hard glare, Chitragupta continued Yamraj's dialogue, “You sorry souls have a once-in-a-million years chance. Each of you made a few choices over the years that forced us to rewrite what was originally meant for you. You took the easy way out too many times.

Pointing at a man in front of me, he continued “You had a choice when the gun was in your hand. You did not have to shoot the police officer.”

“Did you even think that you could have just missed that flight,” he said, pointing to another soul.

“You were out running, from your wife again and all the problems that you were facing,” this to the man I conversed with earlier.

“And you”, a stick pointed to me, “texting while driving??? Look what you did.”

I stood rooted to the ground as Chitragupta glanced from me to the man beside me meaningfully.

"Does he even know who you are, did you tell him while you shared a light? I did not think so, because you have forever been running from your problems Chanda!!!! All your choices have been to run away, never to face them."

"So, all of you are going back to earth to correct your choices. Each one of you has to correct three choices that you made that changed your course of life. We will not tell you where you went wrong. However, you shall be transported back to the time around which these choices came up. You need to figure out what has to be done."

"Once you have corrected your choice, you will feel a light soothing breeze upon yourself, and you shall be transported to the next phase of your lives, where the second twist awaits you. Get the choice right and you go on to the third and final phase," continued St. Peter. "But, remember if the choice is incorrect, the entire thing starts all over again; it is a loop of your own personal Hell then!!!"

Amidst loud protests, I could see that our reactions quite entertained the Gods as they looked at each other gleefully.

"What if we refuse?" I sputtered pretty much to my surprise as well. "What if we don't play your game?" "This is very entertaining for you, right?? Not so 'Holier than thou' now, are we?" I continued. "I mean what is the point of all this? With all due respect, you expect us to fail at this, so what's all the drama?? Just send us to Hell already!!!"

I could feel the daggers sticking out of the eyes of everyone around me. Accusations and pleas did not need to be voiced. I could feel them.

"Oh no!!!! You don't get away with everything so easily now Chanda! You got to pay for your sins. You need to remember the choices and see for yourself what could have been... And then maybe you will have faith," retorted St. Peter.

"Besides," continued Chandragupta, "she does have a few good deeds as well. Those need to be considered. You never know, she might just make the right choice for once."

"So, everyone, be ready. You will feel a tug and a void and be transported to your time of choice. Don't call out to us for any help whatsoever, the

Gods shall not hear you. For once, you guys are really on your own."

"Oh!! And do keep in mind darlings, the choices are not in chronological order," Yamaraj boomed. "What fun would that be? You could be facing your first, second or third place of choice!!! Go Fish!!!!"
Adrenaline rushed through my veins. I have always liked challenges, and have never been able to back down from them, God or no God. I intended to find my place in Heaven.

"Not so fast now Chanda, I believe you owe me an explanation," a low voice whispered on my neck. I could feel the anger in the hold that he had on my wrist. "Where do you think you are going, without telling me how to make sense of what happened to me, because of you!!!?"

CHAPTER 3

THE EXPLANATION

"Care to explain what just happened here," he questioned me.

"Um ahh, I don't know what you're talking about," I stuttered, looking up at him with huge eyes.

"Okay, let's start again. Hi!!! I am Sam or was Sam while I was alive? I live in Mumbai with my wife and kids. We've been married for 28 years, and I was happy. Your turn Chanda."

I turned away, and trying to put some distance between us, muttered "I'm Chanda, live in Mumbai as well, with my kids and have been married 30 years. On the verge of a divorce, I have not been happy for a few years now. I guess, now you know why the Gods picked on me to point out bad choices."

"And", I gulped "I am your moronic driver."

The scene flashed in front of me yet again in slow motion.

It had been an unusually horrid day. My husband of 30 years had once again stayed out the entire night, making me wonder just who he was screwing with this time. Of late things were downhill in my marriage and after spending two years in a gruelling situation, after seeing a few counsellors, we decided to go our separate ways. The children were adults now and could decide for themselves where they wanted to stay.

After finishing my chores, I headed over to my lawyer's office to finally sign the divorce papers. Mr Sethi had been kind enough to explain to me in simple terms all that was written in the agreement. The bastard had decided to sell our house so that he could pay his loans. I would get a place to stay and monthly alimony for as long as I was alive.

So basically, I was losing 30 years of my life, my career was already over long ago, and now the roof over my head was going as well. Dejected and distracted I was on the verge of sealing my fate with a stroke of the pen. Tears streaming down my face, I ran to the car which was thankfully still mine and drove away. I had to get out of there. The papers had soiled my hands, my life sucked and I had no one to blame for this but me.

One hand on the wheel, I fished in my purse to pull out the phone. I had to talk to my sister Tara. I looked at the time and realised Tara would already be asleep in Australia. So, I started texting her to call me as soon as she woke up.

One second, I had my eyes on the phone and the very next instant I was flung forward…

The sound of screeching metal and the smell of burning rubber hit me instantly. Screams resonated from every pore of my body and the metallic taste of blood was on my tongue. I saw white everywhere which turned to red and finally black. In and out of consciousness, I witnessed the accident as if I was standing on one side when it happened. The car was so mangled, that nobody could have been alive inside. Yet somehow, my door was torn apart which gave me room to squeeze out.

Ignoring the blood flowing from my head and mouth, I saw what had happened, and was horrified to see a man, his limbs all twisted under the bonnet of my car! I tried speaking and all that came out was a spurt of red.

“My name is Sam. You have to call my wife. My phone has her number.”

Even before I could ask him his wife's name, life was sucked out of him, and I was staring at his listless eyes. Grey, with a touch of green, vacant, strange yet somehow familiar.

“Miss, are you okay,” somebody asked me as I fell forward.

The moment I hit the ground I assumed I was dead. Then I kept waking and waking. I liked to be unconscious rather than awake. Because when I was awake, I could taste the coppery blood pooling in my mouth. I could feel it grazing my teeth and soaking my tongue. I felt the aching and cracks in my bones. Each crack felt like rocks were burrowing into my skin. I sucked in cramped air, feeling my lungs caving in on themselves. I saw the spots in the corners of my vision, making my head feel like the only thing inside of it was static.

I heard a buzzing noise, filling my ears. I felt like I was there for hours, fading and waking and fading and waking again. My agony was the only thing keeping me alive. It was the only thing I could feel anymore.

That's when I died.

CHAPTER 4

CONFESSION

There was an awkward silence around me, making me realise that I had an audience for my thoughts.

Sam looked at me with a sad expression on his face, his grey-green eyes were as strange as ever. What was it about his eyes?

“Seems you had a rough deal as well,” he said with an apologetic tone. “I am sorry too! I wasn’t looking when I tried crossing the street. I guess if both of us would have been more careful, this could have been avoided.”

“Why were you running away from your wife?" I was equally surprised as him, to air my thoughts aloud. "And why do you seem familiar?” I did not realise I had spoken out loud until his hand on my arm stopped me.

“You don’t remember me, do you?”

I was clueless, as I was caught in his green gaze yet again. Damn, those eyes!!!

I looked at him and looked hard again. There was something familiar about Sam that I could not quite place.

"Have we met before? Do you know me? Who are you??" I did not need to speak out aloud, as he could read my thoughts, as did all the others around me!!! The other side allows telepathy!!!!!

"To get to your earlier question, I have an unhappy marriage..........! Had!" He corrected himself. The exquisite eyes were pretty expressive and I felt I could see right into his soul. Ummm if we still had one that is.

"I've been married 28 years", he said "but I still could not forget the one I could never have." "It was love at first sight for me, and I wanted her right away. I would have walked the extra mile for her, and could have climbed mountains for her!! Hell, I would have brought her the moon as well, if only she knew what she meant to me."

"So what happened?" before I knew it the question was out of my mouth!! Your mind still works the same even though you are dead. The starting of a story always intrigued me. And this was a subject close to my heart. Love. Hadn't I just given up everything for the same reason??

"Maybe it wasn't meant to be", came back the dejected retort. "Or maybe she loved another." The strange look was back in his eyes as he gazed at me intently. He ruled me, he shook me with his look, yet I could not place him.

"Enough about me, let's hear what Chanda is all about."

Chanda is all about loving unconditionally and forsaking everything for the cause. I wanted to tell him but held my tongue. Not that it mattered, as was evident from the lift of his brow. Damn the telepathy, and double damn for me to think like that!!! Wasn't I ever going to get over it all? I mean I was dead for goodness' sake.

"Where do I start? I am Chanda, married for almost 30 years. Married right out of college you could say. It was a love marriage, despite stiff opposition from my family." Pondering deeply I continued, "The day I died was the day I signed my divorce decree."

Nothing could have prepared me for the empathy I saw on his face.

"Don't get me wrong, it has not been all that bad. It was a love marriage, after all, so we were young and very much in love. The entire family, my side was one team, and Tarun and me on one side. Oh, the romance was exhilarating. We could not get enough of each other."

Tarun and I met while I was in college. On the same bus route to my college and his office, we were introduced by common friends and before long things started moving forward. He would wait for me outside the college, I would bunk classes to be with him. Soon life without each other seemed impossible.

By this time, I had finished college and was looking for a job. I wanted to be a costume designer in Bollywood. The fast pace and the million opportunities excited me and I was raving to go. Tarun was very supportive and very possessive at the same time. But I was so in love that I could not see clearly where I was headed. "So what went wrong?"

Before I could collect my thoughts and reply, I sensed someone or something tugging at my arm!!! And then nothingness, a void so deep you probably could not even hear your thoughts.

I was plunged into darkness, only to reemerge a moment later in MY COLLEGE!!!!! This was it!!

The first mistake that I had to rectify!!!!

CHAPTER 5

THE FIRST TURN

I had just finished my classes for the day and was looking forward to going back home. It was the middle of August and the humidity was killing me. New Delhi in August is like sitting in a sauna. The heat is intense with the so-called Monsoons…..humid, sticky and hot.

I usually stayed with my grandparents near the college, but today being Friday I was headed back home to Gurgaon. This was the 90s and my city was unheard of literally. The girls in college did a double-take when I said I was from Gurgaon! 'So you stay in a village?' which was what it was referred to during the pre-mall days.

As I waited for the bus to arrive, I noticed somebody staring at me. Unfazed, I did not return the gaze. This was something one was used to outside a girls' college.

“That guy is looking at you” Seema, my friend said. “I know, and it is now starting to bother me,” I shot back.

I was aware of the stare so much that I had half a mind to go up to him and give him the other piece of my mind!!

Just then our bus pulled up. As I boarded the bus, I glanced back. And the unusual colour of his eyes caught me. Grey with a hint of green in them. ‘Never trust someone with cat eyes!’ I don’t know where I heard this, but the statement had put me into a lot of trouble with my friend in school, so I said nothing.

The weekend went by rather quickly.

For me, the house was now a prison. I hailed from a conservative joint family, where girls could not stay out much. Forever the rebel, the third among four girls, I had put my foot down to go to college in Delhi.

And to avoid commuting, I was asked to stay with my grandparents near the college. Thank God for small mercies!!!

Monday morning saw me back at the bus stop, with my friend on our way to college.

“Oh, my God!! Chanda!!!!!”

“The fledgling is out of her nest!! Welcome to the real world.”

I could have recognized that voice anywhere in the world. My best friend from school was right there, after a gap of almost a year. Sumit had left Gurgaon to go study engineering, and I missed him every day!!!

“Hey, stranger! What brings you here?” I hugged him tight, raising many eyebrows around me. As if I cared, it had been so long since I felt the comfort of his presence. We were inseparable at school, and the only friend from the other sex, who was allowed home! Many times my mother would question me about us.....and I would simply say, he is my best friend: no strings attached, no romantic inclinations; period.

“So, come on, let me introduce you to my friends from college. They are here from down

South to visit the North," he guffawed in his endearing style.

"This, guys, is Chanda, the Demon from school I always talk about!!! As you can see, she has claws," he said, pointing towards me and my fingers. "And this is Raghu, Navin and Tarun, my batchmates at college." I shook hands and looked at them. As soon as I shook hands with the guy called Tarun, something stirred in me. I had a hard time looking away, and like all typical Hindi romance movies that I had seen, and all The Mills and Boons that I had read, everything else faded.

It was as if time did stand still, and there was nothing else around, except me and this guy that I just met. Tarun.

"Oh, how the Mighty fall!!" Exclaimed a voice from far.

"I am witness to the shrew being tamed after all!!" And with a hard pull from someone around me, the spell was broken. It had to be Sumit. Trust him to ruin my moment. "Did you just phase out, Moon?" He only ever called me that when he was up to no good!!!

“Jerk!!” “You had to ruin the moment, didn’t you?” As I smiled at him, I couldn’t but help to see what Tarun's reaction was. Dumbfounded, his face mirrored mine!!!

Love at first sight!!

Little did I realise that the grey-green eyes were observing me all along!!! So began the saga that was to be my life.

Tarun asked me out a few days later, and that year was the best time of my life. I looked forward to class getting over so that I could spend time with him. The chats were never-ending, somehow each day we had so much to talk about. This is from a girl who could not hold a simple conversation for over five minutes. And here I was chatting 19 to the dozen. Unbelievable!!

This went on for a good year or so, but I had yet to mention him to my parents. Soon Tarun started pushing me to get married. He wanted to meet my parents. “We need to break the ice with them.

How would they know about me if you don't tell them?" Are you even serious about me?" His questions made me decide to tell my parents that I was in love.

But how do I tell them? I had never been so open with my parents about anything…forever secretive and a loner, I didn't even know how to take my sister Tara into confidence.

Mustering up as much courage as I could, one weekend I decided to write them a letter and leave it for them to read once I was already back at work. Oh yeah…forgot to mention that I was already interning with a fashion house by this time. College was over and I was waiting for my degree.

I came home the next weekend from my internship and sensed a lot of undercurrents at home. My parents seemed to be on edge and my sister just kept giving me strange glances. Turns out, there was a man and his parents who were coming over that evening. My parents were looking for a match for me, and this family was known to my uncle. He had proposed the match.

CHAPTER 6

THE REFUSAL

"Hi! I am Sameer," a hand jutted out and I all but cringed. "I am Chanda and I am not interested!"

So much for my manners and so much for turning him down politely!

Before he could say anything, I rushed on, "I am sorry. That is not how it was supposed to be said," I stammered. "I am in love with someone and would like to marry him," I tried explaining.

"So what are you doing here, miss?" he asked, stepping closer, "Shouldn't you be with Tarun or Sumit then?" he mocked.

I was aghast and my eyes cast down all this while, flew to his face! A glimpse of the strangest green caught my gaze before he looked away.

"Yes, I know about them. But the question is, do you? Which one loves you, and who do you love? Do you even know that for sure?"

While I let these strange comments sink in, the rest of the girl-meets-boy jing bang was around us. Like the coward and hypocrite that I felt at that moment, I kept my head down and zoned out to the questions and the chatter around me.

As we, the girls' side was about to leave, a chit was thrust into my hand, with a gruff "call me" whispered for my ears only!

As I looked back, the green-grey eyes stared back at me, yet again. And yet again, I could not place them.

All hell broke loose, the minute we got home!!!!

My parents had read the letter that I had left for them and were not happy with this turn of events. And so began the ordeal of a modern-day Juliet!

I was shifted to my aunt's place, where my cousin was assigned the duty of making sure I got to work and back home on time. I was dropped off at work and then picked up as soon as I finished!!

Ummm, did they not know about the invention of the Telephone? I wondered. Or did they think that I was so brainless, that I would just sit it out until they decided what had to be done?

Taking matters into my own hands, I called up the number that had been thrust into my hands when I met Green Eyes……

"I have been waiting to hear from you. What took you so long?"

"How do you even know who it is on the other end?" I asked, feeling stupid and a bit self-conscious. I was about to refuse this guy, yet he recognized my voice!!

"Nobody has this number except you," said Sameer with a smile in his voice. Well, that did put me and my stupidity in place!!!!

"So, is it a yes?" He asked hopefully.

"I am sorry Sameer, it's not you, it's me," and I started my well-rehearsed speech. I had always been a people pleaser and tried to make everyone happy. But this here, was a situation where there had to be a choice and I was not comfortably upsetting someone at my expense!!!

To my surprise, he seemed rather prepared for it. A lot of ifs and buts did take place and a lot of what ifs as well.

“I’ll step back, but only if you tell me who it is that won your heart. I think I need to know who bested me.”

With a sigh of relief and a light heart I whispered, “Tarun.”

I could sense the disbelief in his voice over the phone, as he started to say something.

But then, there was this shrill noise all around me…I felt a tug on my arm and then I was falling into nothingness!!

CHAPTER 7

MY HELL LOOP

After what seemed like an eternity, I found myself back at The Gates of my college yet again!!!!!

I HAD MADE THE WRONG CHOICE!!!!

The explicit words that came out of my mouth would have earned me boxed ears if my mother had heard them.

“That guy is looking at you,” once again I heard my friend Seema say to me. I was too flustered to say anything at all! While this was an ordinary day for Seema, it wasn’t for me. I had already lived this day many years ago!!

“You look sick,” she commented again. “Are you okay?”

I simply nodded since I had no words to describe what I was going through. How do I tell her that I had travelled back in time, a good 20-25 years? How do I tell her that I had made a mistake that I was supposed to rectify and that I had no clue as to what the mistake was?

I went back home yet again and faced the entire situation over again. My parents still wanted me to meet this boy that they liked, they still wanted to get me married off, and I was still as clueless as before about my mistake.

Was I supposed to say yes to this random guy that my parents had picked out? What would life be like with him?? What if I still ended up in this loop yet again in 2020?

Did the pandemic as well depend on my bloody choice!!!!! I sure was not shifting to China to have a say in this to find out!

And then came the fateful day that I was dreading. The meeting with Sameer and his family.

I had a plan in mind. One which I wanted to discuss with Tarun. But that had to wait until I was back at work.

And so...

CHAPTER 8

THE PLAN

"Hi! I am Sameer," a hand jutted out and I all but cringed once again.

"I am Chanda," I replied as demurely as I could. And as easy as that, my plan was set into action!

The conversation with Sameer was quite interesting. He was in the hotel industry and had a lot of interesting tales to tell. And again what drew me were his eyes, the green shining when he laughed, and the grey pre-dominant when he was thinking. For a minute I thought that I would change my plan, and agree to marry him!!!

As if sensing my thoughts, he gave me a very strange look that was questioning and accepting at the same time.

My plan was quite simple if all the dominoes fell as I had envisioned them. I wanted to buy time here with Sameer before I could do anything. I was so sure that my mistake, later on, had been hurting him when I outright refused him.

So I had to make sure that he was fine and in sync with me, when I called the shots and told him, or rather cajoled him into refusing to marry me. But at the same time, I had been spiralling into this Hell loop, as soon as I said that I was in love with Tarun.

Which meant that maybe Tarun wasn't the one for me!!!!

But I loved him with all my heart! How was it even possible that we were not meant to be together? Yet knowing what I knew was going to happen 30 years down the line, I did begin to question myself. I had signed my divorce papers when I got killed! Was it worthwhile to just give it all away? Will I still be divorced in the future? Will I be in a better place? What about my beautiful kids!!!

I wouldn't trade them for anything in the world!! Not even my happiness, or my life!

Sameer and I spent almost an hour chatting like we were old friends. And then he asked me "So who is it, Chanda?" "Tarun or Sumit?"

I was prepared!!

"Um, I don't know for sure. I thought that I was in love with Tarun," I said and told him about the letter that I had written to my parents.

"And now?"

I could see the question in his eyes, even before he uttered the words. "I don't know!"

Man, I was good!! I could have patted my own back as I put in as much self-doubt as I could in that simple statement!

"I think I need more time to decide". The final domino is in place for this section!!

"Let's give it some time. Who knows you might just fall in love with me!" The grin on his face held a promise that I was unwilling to accept at that moment.

"I guess!"

Soon it was time to leave, and unlike the first time, he gave me a piece of paper with his number in full view of the family. Call me, he said, winking at me with a smile.

Knowing what was in store for me once we got home, I smiled at him, and then at my parents, trying to give them some hope that I wasn't so far gone! Plus, hoping that they would not see through me. Especially Mom!! She was as perceptive as I would be when I have my kids. We mothers just know when our kids are lying.

As soon as we got home, this time around I rushed into an explanation even before we were in through the door.

CHAPTER 9

DOMINOES IN PLACE

“Mom, Dad, hear me out first," I pleaded.

“I may have made a mistake,” not to sound like I was lying, “I had a good time today with Sameer,” I continued. “He seems to be a very stable guy and is very well-read as well.”

My parents exchanged a look I had come to relate with the scenario that they were not convinced and that they smelt a rat somewhere.

“I was hasty in telling you about Tarun I think. The problem is that I have never dated many boys, so I probably thought that I was in love.”

Didn’t sound very convincing!

“How about, I shift to Massi’s house, to get away from him for a bit?” They were contemplating this, I knew, “That way I can then spend some time with Sameer.”

My Ace card was out on the table!!

But the fool that I was, had no idea what being a parent meant, and how they are far ahead of you and your scheming mind and are always ready for anything you throw at them!!

"You will stay here and commute from here to work with your cousin." This statement was final from my father.

A spanner in the wheel for sure, but I could work with that. I had to be patient, I knew. But the important thing was for me to speak with Tarun! How do I manage that?

Out came a card that was closer to me than anyone, in terms of being like me. Sumit!

"Hey, you! What's up?!"

"Oye, eid ka chand!! Where are you? Haven't heard from you in ages." His easy banter reduced me to tears. I hadn't broken down in front of anyone as yet, but hearing Sumit's voice over the phone was like opening a tap.

"I need you here, now Sumit," I wailed over the phone.

CHAPTER 10

SELF DOUBT

The evening saw me sitting cradled in Sumit's arms. My eyes were swollen from crying and I was a wreck. His shirt was soaked to the skin with my tears, and he must have had several cramps in his arms by now, holding me to himself as tightly as he could.

"So what next?" he asked me, carefully lifting my chin to gaze into my eyes.

"I don't know as yet," I sniffled. "All I know is that I don't want to be divorced later in life." I was as surprised as Sumit, by this statement that had suddenly poured out of my mouth.

"Why would you think like that?" Sumit reprimanded me. "You love Tarun, and he loves you, right? So I am sure you will work things out. And who does not have nitty-gritty squabbles?? I mean, haven't you seen your parents fight, ever?"

"Plus, you guys are not even married yet, and you are already thinking of a divorce as if you know what's in store for you!!"

How I wished I could make him understand!! I sounded crazy even to myself, how the hell was I supposed to make my best friend understand and accept that I was already dead, and had come back from the future…literally from the land of the dead!

Wiping my eyes with finality, the decision was made, and I faced Sumit. "Listen. I have a plan and you have to help me with it. This guy Sameer, knows about Tarun and you."

"What about me?" A strange look in his eyes, Sumit asked me perplexed. "How do I end up being dragged into your shit always, Moon??

"Get used to it, Jerk!!" I smiled for the first time that day.

"This shit will hit the ceiling soon, and you will be there all along. You will always be there all through my life." My smug statement had quite an effect on him, for I could see Sumit turning away his face. He always did that when his emotions were too raw for him to handle!

“So,” I continued, giving him a minute to gather himself. “I have to spend time with this Sameer so that it seems as if I am genuinely interested in him.”

“The problem is Tarun,” I whispered. “I can’t meet him and I can’t speak with him! The guard around me is very tight for me to slip. I need you to meet with him and explain the whole situation to him. And make sure that he understands what I am trying to do.”

Sumit looked at me in bafflement.

“You mean to say that he knows nothing about what has transpired already?”

"Are you crazy woman!!” he all but shouted at me. “You do realise what this would look like to him? Hell, I have this feeling that you are about to dump him! And you want me to be the bearer of this news flash!” He stared at me with trepidation.

Both of us knew that Tarun could be very short-tempered and easy to jump the gun! He was quick to jump to conclusions as well. A bit volatile, but a guy with a huge heart! He would do anything for the people he loved, mess with him, and you could be an enemy for life.

And here I was, the girl he loved, putting him in a situation he knew nothing about, and in the process risking his friendship with Sumit as well, since he was my chosen messenger!

No wonder I died that day! If only I had died and gone straight to Hell, or Heaven!! Such a heartless manipulator I was turning out to be.

"Do you even realise what you are doing, Chanda?"

A question that was now beginning to haunt me, came from this one guy who understood me completely. And this hurt like nothing ever had.

"Please trust me, Sumit, this will work for all of us and will make life much better at a later stage."

"What are you even talking about? Just live in the present Chanda. You will spoil this time that you have to worry about the future! Who knows what's in store for us 10 years down the line?"

"I do!! And I am trying to make it better," I screamed even before I could stop myself.

"Please just go and talk to Tarun and try and make him see reason!" I all but shoved him out the door, before I completely lost my mind.

What I was doing was not right. I could feel it in my bones. So how do I explain this to myself?

This plan it seemed to me now was doomed to fail. I could not just play with Sameer, Tarun and Sumit's emotions all at the same time! This wasn't me. I was better than this.

From where I was standing, now just one thing made sense to me. Either I say yes to Sameer, thus changing my choice so that I could escape the loop that would follow if I chose Tarun yet again. Or then I simply live in this loop over and over again!!!!

What would life with Sameer be like? Would I still have a chance at happiness, knowing that I loved somebody else? Will I ever be able to love Sameer as much as I loved Tarun…will I still end up divorced and dead in 2020? There was no way of knowing that now, was there??

I needed to talk to Tarun and Sumit. I had to tell them what was happening to me. But it wasn't that simple. Could I even tell them about the fact that I had come back from the future? I mean, it did not make sense to me still, so how was I supposed to make them understand? But I could not keep them in the dark any longer.

CHAPTER 11

THE FINAL MEETING

The following week saw me back at work with no mental peace. It was as if the Gods were making sure that I messed up. My professional life was also all out, with my superiors rejecting my designs.

"Attire for the main lead, Chanda!!! Not a bloody sidekick!" my boss yelled at me for the umpteenth time.

"What's going on? Have you lost interest in your work or what? Getting married, are you?" jeered my much-hated colleague Vaibhav...he went on to become a famous designer at a later stage. At that point, he was just an intern like me and always managed to rub me the wrong way.

"Vaibhav, listen, I need a favour," I spoke up even as I was formulating yet another plan.

"Can you cover for me, please? I have to meet my friend urgently and you are right, I might be getting married sooner than I had wished for," I added with no joy in my tone.

For once, he probably saw the sense of urgency over me, and let his good side show. "Will you come back or do I cover for you tomorrow as well?" he tried to joke.

"I'll be here in the morning." My word was very important to me, if I said something, I stood by it. So imagine the enormity of what I was about to do. I was about to go back on my word given to Tarun. I just wished yet again, that I could die right there and escape this situation altogether.

Chitragupta had been right when he said that I ran away from problems without facing them. Well, time to prove him wrong, and stand up for once.

I gave a missed call at Tarun's office, which meant that he had to call back ASAP. The cell phone was still a few years away and this was the norm in the early 90s. Normal for me.

I practically grabbed the phone off the hook as soon as it rang. "Get Sumit and meet me at the usual place in 45 minutes," I spoke quietly and quickly since personal phone calls were not allowed in the fashion house.

An hour later I saw myself sitting opposite both Tarun and Sumit, a look of disbelief on both their faces.

"So you mean to say, that you are going to marry this Sameer guy, who you don't even know properly, forget about me, and then what!" I could sense the anger seething under Tarun's strangely calm voice.

"I don't know!! Divorce him probably and come back to you?"

"Are you crazy Chanda!" two sets of eyes glared at me angrily, as I practically covered my ears against the accusing tone in both the voices.

"Why can't you simply refuse?" I'll apply for a marriage licence and we can get married in a matter of a month." Tarun all but shouted. "I cannot lose you!!"

"Look, my parents have practically given us their blessings. Maybe I can ask them to meet with your parents and work things out? Or better still, let me go meet your Dad and plead with him." This coming from the self-respecting Tarun was too much for me to handle. I was being crushed between the two men that I loved the most. My father, who had never said no to me, and Tarun, who I had envisioned spending my life with.

"Why not just agree to an engagement for now?" Sumit had been quiet all this while, and while we were drowning in self-pity and anger, his mind was working out different scenarios. "You need to buy time to figure out what to do next, right? So agree to an engagement and then say that you would like to complete your graduation and work for a bit before marriage."

"Don't rush into anything, Moon." Sumit was probably the calmest one at that moment.

"Take your time, think things over and then decide what you want to do. There is only one life, my dear. Do not mess it up."

I wish I could just have told him. I already messed it up!

CHAPTER 12

THE DILEMMA

That was the final meeting between Tarun and me. We decided that we could not risk being seen together. Yet another plan was now in action. The meeting with Tarun and Sumit, brought me little solace, knowing that they were by my side. But Sumit's words still ran around in my mind. Despite his idea, he was not really convinced that I should get engaged to buy more time. He was still in the good books of my parents, and so he became our Homing Pigeon – The messenger.

A fortnight later, I got engaged to Sameer in a very simple affair.

The ring felt like a dead weight on my finger, the smile on my face seemed to have been etched by a shard of glass, and I could taste blood on my tongue from having bitten my lips so many times!

I had never realised what the term, the sound of a broken heart meant until that day. While the family was happy and joyous and celebrating, the man beside me was also quiet. His smile not quite reaching his grey-green eyes.

"Chanda, are you okay? Can I get you something?" He seemed concerned. But for what it was worth, I did blame him as well. He could also have refused this engagement. I mean, who in their right mind would like to marry a girl who said that she loved someone else!!!! Chivalrous, my foot!!

"Arree Sameer Sahib, she still has a bit of time before she becomes your wife! Let me look after her for a while, before you whisk her away." The familiar voice broke my heart all over again.

With a tear in my eye, I flung myself into Sumit's arms. The only person here who knew what I was going through.

"She'll always be your friend, Sumit, no matter what. I am marrying her, not ruling over her," laughed Sameer. The boys exchanged a glance that made no sense to me, but Sumit just looked at me and laughed, a strange thought dawning upon him.

"He knows what you are up to, Moon," Sumit whispered. "Don't ask me how, but I just know it. So be careful," he warned before handing over my hand to Sameer's.

A month went by, and I went along with this farce of an engagement.

In all honesty, Sameer tried hard to keep me happy whenever he asked me out. I tried keeping my Mom and Dad happy by going out with him. But was I happy?? I did not know. My heart still yearned for Tarun, but my circumstances were such that I could not be with him.

I had been raised in a religious family and grudgingly believed in a higher Authority.

Don't get me wrong. I had faith. But these rituals of a havan or spending hours in front of an idol seemed like a waste of time to me. I could never do it. Even in my former life, I was not a person who followed religion by the book. I prayed when I felt like it. But I always thanked the Higher Authority for every day that went by. I was thankful to be alive.

Anyway, I was now spending a lot of time with Sameer, and strangely enough I began to wonder if he was supposed to be my choice, after all. Was this the mistake that I had to correct? Did I have to choose Sameer over Tarun to get through the loop that the Gods had created for me? Was this even right?

I had to speak with Sumit. He had told me that Tarun had gone away for an office trip and would be back in a couple of days. And I had decided that once he got back, I would finally put forth the entire truth to him, however bizarre it sounded. There was no other way.

Yet again, I was thinking about myself, what mattered to me, what was making me uncomfortable and what seemed like a life-changing decision...and at that moment getting myself out of the rut that was soon to follow, subject to my choice, was inevitable. I had to reverse it.

I would agree to marry Sameer.

I had to tell this to Tarun myself. Sumit could not be the one to give this news to him. It had to be me.

“Let's go out tonight, Chanda, I want to discuss something very important with you.” This sentence from Sameer as soon as he called me a day later had me in jitters. I think I already knew what he wanted to ask me.

“Sure,” I mustered up all my courage and asked him. “Do you want to go for a drive or a quiet dinner?” I crossed my fingers and wished for him to say dinner. At least we will be surrounded by people then.

“I’ll pick you up and then let’s go to the club.” The club was the deadest place that I had ever been to!!! Nothing interesting ever happened there.

I had to do this. It was about time that this matter got resolved. However painful it was, it seemed that I would now have to meet Tarun the very next day and try to explain the situation to him and make him accept my decision.

The decision of marrying Sameer.

The evening found me nervous, and edgy.

Small talk seemed impossible for me today! This was the biggest decision of my life and I was unnaturally silent. “All okay with you?” inquired Sameer. I just nodded and looked away. Words seemed impossible.

Soon we were seated opposite each other and already looking at the menu. I have been a foodie all my life, yet there was nothing that interested me at that moment. My nervousness got through to Sameer, who ordered for both of us. As soon as we were alone, he gently took my hand and kissed it.

This was the first time he had done something like this, and this gesture had a sense of finality. I looked at him questioningly.

“Chanda, I need to say something,” he whispered.

The look in his eyes was one that I had never seen before. Trepidation, anxiety, nervousness, and fear all mixed together and chased each other one after the other.

“I think I have made a decision that is going to affect both of us. Not just now, even in 2020.”

Horror dawned on me as the words sunk into my now clouded brain!

CHAPTER 13

THE CHOICES WE MAKE

"You have never been alone in this journey you see. I travelled back with you as well, since our lives have always been entangled."

And then, like the domino effect, the cards started falling, one on top of the other.

The grey-green eyes watching me at the bus stop.

The sense of being watched even while I was chatting with Sumit. The time when I met Tarun for the first time.

And then, finally when I killed him, Sameer! It had been him all along!

"But how?" I spluttered, "How long have you been stalking me?" I asked bewildered.

"I wasn't," he retorted back quickly. "I was trying to get out of this loop, just like you. My loop started much before yours. When you met me at The Gates, I had already been dead several times over. Each time it was somebody else, but then I saw that each time, under any circumstance I was stuck on you."

"The first loop came up when I saw you on the bus, talking to Sumit and Tarun. Haven't been able to forget you even now. So I decided to see where you stayed, who you were, and what you liked etc. I had lost my heart to you then and wanted you to love me as well, and be in my life forever. So I asked my parents to talk to you."

This revelation was like a tempest in an already stormy sea. I was flabbergasted.

"The second time I got caught in the loop was when I watched you at the bus stop. I thought that if I met you and introduced myself to you, things would work out differently."

"Each time you were out of my reach!" he continued sadly.

I could do nothing except sympathise with him. This is what was happening to me as well. I was running after something, or rather someone, who may always be wrong for me.

"The final time when I saw you behind the wheel of the car, I could have stepped back, but something made me step forward. One last try I thought to myself. And if it still does not work out, well I just would have had to let go."

I finally understood all the strange glances that I had been getting from him, ever since I got into this loop. His sentiments mirrored mine, as I had as well decided to let go. But now, the person who was to be my anchor seemed in a dubious situation as well.

"I came here today to tell you that I have asked my parents to back out of this marriage alliance," he stopped me when I started to say something. "I have had enough of it, Chanda, and have finally understood that we are not destined to be together. The only way forward for me is to let go of my fascination for you. I realise now, that maybe this passion that I felt for you back then, may have been the cause of all my problems. I was trying to attain the Moon." He smiled sadly and with finality.

Now that he had made his decision, I expected him to be swept away from me. But he stayed put.

"I need you to accept my decision before I can move on, Chanda. But before you accept my choice, just tell me who it is going to be this time. I just have to know before I disappear from your life forever."

I looked at him with renewed emotions. The man in front of me loved me as much as I loved Tarun. His eyes, the ones that always got me confused, were brimming with tears and an emotion I knew very well.

He did not want to let go, but he was going to, because I loved another. This was not something I would have done. Me, being the self-centred being that I was, would have just grabbed this opportunity and tried convincing the other person how right I was for him.

But not Sameer. He turned out to be a thorough gentleman, I thought.

Tarun, on the other hand, had been hurt when I told him my plan, but did he fight for me?

Will he ever fight for me? I was forced to think. Maybe, just maybe, Sameer was the one for me?

I had to find out. Maybe my loop led me to him finally. But would I be able to forget Tarun? Would I be able to love Sameer as much, or maybe more?

"Chanda," he said again, "please put me out of my misery. I don't think I can go back again. I have had enough of these loops. Each one turns out to be more difficult than the last."

With finality in my mind, I turned to him and slowly looked at him.

"It was going to be you, Sameer," I whispered.

CHAPTER 14

A TWIST IN THE TALE

And just like that, both of us were whisked away into oblivion. “The wrong choice again, I guess,” Sameer whispered softly. “Does it have to be?” I questioned him.

“What if we can make this work? What if we just ask to see Yamraj Ji again? Aren’t you tired of giving me up all the time?” I smiled as I said the last sentence, trying to ease his tension a bit.

No sooner that the thought crossed my mind, we found ourselves at The Gates this time.

Perplexed, we looked at each other. This was not how it was supposed to be. Where was the loop? Why were we here?

“So we meet again,” boomed the loud voice of Yamraj. “Chitragupta? Are they done with the loops or what? Show me their files,” he continued, as confused as us.

"Sir, there has been a new development," Chitragupta muttered under his breath, looking at the files he had in hand.

So now, we had files…I would have thought that the Gods would have progressed to data cards by now, or pen drives.

"Chanda is starting to show signs of change. She is not just thinking about herself now. Seems that her heart is changing," bewildered Chitragupta looked at me, then at Sameer, and then at The Dark Lord himself.

"What! She had a heart transplant or what?" Guffawed Yamraj ji, quite to my annoyance.

I could hear the snide comments running through their minds.

"Hmmmm."

"Oh! Okay!"

"Well, let's see what we have here," Yamraj and Chitragupta pondered amongst themselves, leaving both Sameer and me on tenterhooks.

"But that's not meant to be, Sir!" Chitragupta seemed a bit indignant.

"Quite!" Thundered Yamraj ji. "I know that!!! I wrote it! It shall be, all in good time. But if she changes, which seems highly unlikely, then this can happen as well. We are allowed to rewrite destinies sometimes, you know."

Whatever I was hearing, or rather trying to hear, was a bit confusing. What was not meant to be, I could very well imagine. It was the wrong choice, after all. But then why were we at The Gates, instead of spiralling back to some point in our lives again. Sameer seemed just as confused as me, but he refrained from saying anything at all. As if, he had already reconciled himself to another loop.

"All right children! Listen up!" The Dark Lord finally addressed us.

"This is quite unexpected and unprecedented, this is not how things are to be. But," looking at me he continued, "I see something good happening in Chanda. She seems to be changing her ways."

"And you do know that when someone changes for good or for worse, us Gods are forced to reevaluate your files."

"You are free to get on with your lives," smiling Chitragupta stepped forward and gave us a gentle nudge. "You will now find yourselves married and leading a new life," he said. "After all, we cannot have Chanda change her mind again!!"

CHAPTER 15

MARRIED AND HAPPY, OR WAS ?

As I felt my feet touch the ground, my heart filled with trepidation. Where the hell had I landed this time? And would I really be changing my mind again? From what Chitragupta said, that was quite a possibility.

"Hey Chanda wake up!!! It's time." I felt his soft touch upon my back and all but melted against him. This felt familiar and I wanted that touch. In fact, I had given myself to him. The first man that I ever slept with – my husband.

I opened my eyes and found myself in a strange bed. Yet I somehow knew that this was Sameer's home. It just seemed rather strange to suddenly have these memories of being married already.

We had been married for almost two years now. My parents had been very happy that finally I had found a good match and that I had done what they wanted for me all along. To get married into an upper middle class family. Money had always been an issue for us, so I don't actually blame them for thinking like that. The wedding had been a quiet affair with a few friends and family.

Sumit had been there.

I remembered the look on his face when I told him that I was getting married to Sameer. The disbelief and disappointment was very evident. But I had no way of telling him why.

"This is for the best Sumit, my parents would never agree to me marrying Tarun."

This statement from my mouth sounded hollow and made me cringe even now. Had I turned into somebody who was only looking out for herself? Or were my feelings for Tarun not deep enough? Maybe I was thinking of Sameer, who had spent loop after loop trying to win my love. I had no way of telling my best friend all of this. He wouldn't judge me, I knew, but would he understand?

But what Sumit had said was something that kept me awake even now.

"What about me? Did you never notice? Are you so dense, Chanda, or simply heartless!"

And then he kept his distance from me. Never once giving me a chance to ask him what he had meant.

He came to my wedding, but after that it had been months that I had not seen him as well. And slowly, I began adapting to my new life.

Slowly and steadily, I adapted myself to my married life. Sameer was an only child and was by default, things at home began to go as per what the 'Dulhan' wanted. We stayed with his parents for a few months. But soon we shifted into our own apartment. Frankly, I did not mind staying with his parents. Having been raised in a joint family, I was used to having people around me.

Having said that, setting up a new house, with everything as per what you like and want was an altogether different ball game. For the first time in my life, I was looking out for somebody else as well, instead of just me. I guess marriage does do that to you. Consciously, or unconsciously, you end up making decisions keeping your spouse in mind.

Soon enough we were already celebrating our first anniversary together. I was happy. The loops are a distant memory. How they were to come by and haunt me yet again was another story. But right now, at this very moment I was elated.

I wanted to share the news with Sameer as soon as possible. I had been meaning to tell him for the past few days, but it never did seem like the right moment. To be honest, I was a bit embarrassed as well?

How do you tell your husband that you were both going to be parents soon?! I had only just found out a week ago, and I wanted to break the news in a nice surrounding, over a quiet dinner and probably my last glass of wine for the next several months.

"Come on Chanda!! We're going to be late," Sameer did not have much patience.

"I'm awake!!! Stop yelling," I replied flippantly.

"We have to be at the restaurant in about an hour, and the traffic is going to be crazy!!"

"Who holds a party on a week-day?" I whined.

"Chanda please!" The frustration was becoming evident in his voice. With a chuckle, I hugged him before going into the closet, "Just kidding."

It was a Tuesday morning, and there was this breakfast 'thing' that we had to go to. I still did not know what exactly this thing was.

Pretty soon we were dressed and out of the house. We decided to take just one car, and I would just take a cab to work later. I hated driving, especially in the morning rush hour.

"Don't you want to know where we are headed?" asked Sameer, as I seated myself comfortably in the car.

"Some showroom opening I guess," after all a havan is the only thing that happens early in the morning.

"I always knew you were so damn intelligent!" The easy banter between us was growing on me, and now I found everything about Sameer so endearing. The initial weeks had been a bit tough. Especially when he touched me. I hadn't realised that for a marriage to work, the chemistry between the two has to be good too. And what we had between us—Sameer and I—was nothing short of a raging fire. Even now, we could not get enough of each other! His kisses awakened in me a desire I never knew. His touch sent me spiralling up, out into the universe. The damn Hell loops were put to shame with the kind of loop he put me into.

And to top it all we were going to be parents!! I just couldn't wait to tell Sameer. Tonight for sure, I thought to myself, making plans for the evening already. I was about 4 weeks along, so had no signs to show as yet. But soon enough my body would start changing, and morning sickness might set in. All the same, I was elated.

"Chanda, are you happy with me?" The question caught me off guard and I wondered what had gotten into Sameer.

"Why do you ask this Sameer? Of course, I am happy! Want me to show you how much?" I teased with a grin as I inched down my hand towards his pants.

"Hey! Come on! I am serious here," he put my hand away with a smile in his voice.

"I ask, because we will be meeting a few of your close friends in a few minutes from now." "Seema and Tarun have opened up a new office and studio, and that is where we are headed," he explained.

CHAPTER 16

A REVELATION

"Wait! What!" I was dumbfounded! Seema and Tarun? When did that happen? Nobody told me! Seema and I had been practically together everyday at college, and I knew that Sumit and Tarun were close.

Sumit also did not say anything to me.

And Seema!!! Why, that snake…she had to get hooked up to Tarun! Of all the people! What was she thinking?

I suddenly felt all riled up and was at a loss of words. I could not explain the feeling that was engulfing me. I was happy with Sameer, so why was I bothered with what Tarun or Seema did?

Yet, how come I was the one in the dark? We used to be a team, Seema and I. She knew I was in love with Tarun, and yet, the moment I am out of the picture she makes her moves. How could she! And Sumit! He had a lot to answer for.

“Does this mean you still have lingering feelings for Tarun?” Sameer looked at me, stunned!

Shit! I had forgotten….ever since the loops, we could actually read each other’s minds. There were no boundaries between us it seemed. We just had to be in the same room and we could read the others' minds as well as them telling us exactly what they were thinking. Word for bloody word!!

“Sameer please!” I pleaded. “It just seems too much to handle, that’s all! I never thought that Seema had any romantic notions about Tarun. She never said anything ever, so I am just stunned.”

Thankfully we pulled up in front of our destination, and the conversation was dropped for the moment. I knew this would come up again, and I was not looking forward to it.

“Hey Sameer! And Sameer’s New Moon!”

It could be none other than Sumit! Was I glad to hear the familiar, yet different name that he had for me? New Moon? Really? Had I changed so much, or was it his way of showing sarcasm again? I did not want to dwell on this thought, for obvious reasons!

"Hey! Same Old Jerk! I called out cheekily, hoping to get a decent smile out of him. He hugged me as was our ritual, yet it felt restrained. I felt him holding back, and I did not like it. Something had changed, but I could not figure out what.

Pretty soon I saw Tarun and Seema walk up to us. Seema seemed a bit nervous around me.

"Congratulations you two!" I tried putting Seema at ease with my smile, and to show her that we were good. "So happy for the both of you," I further added while looping in Tarun along with Seema.

"Ummmm, Chanda, can I talk to you for a minute?" Tarun hesitated slightly, looking at Seema sheepishly.

"Actually, I'd like to talk to the both of you." I was as surprised as Seema and Tarun, when I said this, and proceeded to walk into the new studio,—Seema's workplace— which I guessed with all the design books and drafts laid out.

"Chanda, I would like to explain what happened," said Tarun once we were out of earshot of the rest of the family and friends.

"Tarun, Seema—I really am very happy for you guys," I tried putting their minds at rest. "I know that we were close at one time Tarun, but I don't expect you to keep waiting for me, you know. I am married now, and happy!"

This seemed to anger Tarun. His eyes started getting cloudier and darker by the seconds.

"And you thought it was okay to leave me in the lurch?" He whispered harshly.

"Do you even realise what you put me through? Imagine me hurrying back after my trip, only to find out that you got engaged to that man! Whatever happened to just an engagement to buy time? Wasn't that the angle we were going to play?"

I stepped back in shock. He was right! In my haste to get out of the loops, I probably completely forgot to give him an explanation.

"Did his wealth blind you to love Chanda?"

I didn't even know when I slapped him. The sound that echoed in the room stunned all three of us!

"I just wanted to wish you both well. I realise that I have wronged you, Tarun. But that statement you just made? That was a very low blow…"

Having said that, I simply walked out, eyes bright with unshed tears and my head held high!! I did not owe him any explanation now. I had always prided myself for never caring about materialistic comforts, but to have a good friend think otherwise, simply broke me a bit.

Tarun would have been the wrong choice, I reckoned, thanking my lucky stars that I ended up with Sameer.

CHAPTER 17

AN HONEST CONVERSATION

"How have you been, Sumit? It's been a long time! We don't see you around these days?" Sameer spoke out my thoughts, as I approached him planning on pleading a headache to get out of the gathering.

"Been busy, man! Have a new job which takes up most of my time, you know. Plus the family is after me as well to get married. So..."

Sumit seemed on edge, and I wondered for the umpteenth time what was wrong? Had I done something to hurt him?

"So, did you find a match yet?" I asked him excitedly. "Oh wow! It will be fun, your wedding!"

"She married another...my match." Sumit's words shook me to the core.

The look he gave me was something I had never ever seen in his eyes before. This could not be happening to me! It could not be…

I stared at him in horror, as it slowly dawned on me, just exactly what he meant. This really could not be happening…he was my best friend! How could I have missed the signs?

He being by my side always.

Making sure I was okay, whenever I was away from him. Rushing to meet me, as soon as he got home from college. Always taking care of me, getting into fights for me.

As our eyes met yet again, he saw that I finally got it. He loved me.

He simply smiled at me sadly as he turned away. I reached out a hand to grab him, my throat constricting as my tears slowly gave way.

"Wanna sit down for a bit Chanda," I felt Sameer gently leading me to a few chairs, and seating me down.

"No! I all but screamed! I wanna talk to him. Please Sameer! I need to know." I pleaded with him.

"Relax, darling. Not here. Not like this. I promise, we will talk to him." Sameer's words brought me little solace.

Soon enough, Sameer made excuses for the both of us as we left the showroom. He was lost in thoughts, me in a daze, still trying to comprehend what I had just discovered.

"You knew!!"

"You did not know?"

No sooner than we were seated in the car, both Sameer and I burst out together.

"Of course, I knew Chanda! It's written all over his face! How could you have not known? I mean you practically spent every waking minute with Sumit, and yet you never knew that he loved you!! What kinda friend have you been?"

This outburst was too much for me to handle. I was in shock clearly, and I still thought that there was some mix up somewhere. How could this be possible? How could I have missed such an important aspect in my best friend's life?

He loved me, yet he never once tried getting me for himself. Never once let me on to his feelings;

making me make decisions that I saw fit pertaining to my life, while all this while I could have actually fallen for him as well.

"So now, are you in love with Sumit then?" Sameer asked me sadly. "And what was all that talk about, with Tarun?" Damn the telepathy!!

"Why did you really marry me, Chanda?"

"Are you still planning on divorcing me to be with Tarun?"

"Now that Tarun is with Seema, do you think you'll be able to get away with ruining four lives?"

"And what about Sumit?"

Sameer was getting angrier and angrier as he spoke.

"Let's just get home and talk it out," I spoke up with a renewed resolve. I had decided to tell Sameer about all that had happened before we got married. About my now-seemingly absurd plan, of marrying him and then divorcing him, about how I had asked Sumit to help me, and how he had reacted, and how I just got married to him, without breaking off anything with Tarun finally.

Reliving all those moments, I did feel ashamed. I had lied to three wonderful men, who all loved me in their own ways. I did not have a right to play with any of them. And that is exactly what I had done.

Tarun loved me from the day he met me on that fateful bus, and I fell for him like a ton of bricks. I wasn't sure if that had been a mature decision. I was, after all, young and fresh out of college.

Sameer, also claimed to have been in love with me since he saw me. His love had transcended a lot of boundaries. He had apparently been in a few loops, all so that he could have me. Was that love?? Sounded a bit selfish to me. Something that I am sure I would have done as well.

Sumit…what can I say about him? He had loved me silently, without me even knowing about it. No expectations, no promises, just pure, selfless undying love. He loved me so much that my happiness took precedence over everything else.

“If you've done evaluating us men, would you like to get out of the car now?” I didn't even realise that we were home and Sameer had the door open for me.

Neither of us went to work that day.

The entire day passed with us sitting in different rooms or walking on eggshells around each other. I guess Sameer was waiting for me to start the conversation. And I had suddenly lost my voice as well as my courage. So much for being a grown woman, who knows her mind and who had the guts to plan something so remotely stupid as to get married, get divorced and then remarry her love!!!

Not once had I factored in any such thing as a change of heart, or the universe conspiring against my ‘foolproof’ plan!!

“We need to talk, Sameer,” I said as I got us both a cup of tea each. The day had gone by and I knew that we needed to resolve this.

“What is left to say, Chanda,” he replied gruffly. “It just seems that you deceived me right from the start! I was willing to let you go, I had finally come to terms with the fact that you and I are never meant to be. So why did you decide to marry me?"

"I had a change of heart!" I all but shouted at him. "You told me that you had been through several loops to get to me, each time going back yet again! I was moved by that fact." Tears streaming down my face, I continued "I had been in the loop already and realised that Tarun was the wrong choice, and so I was convinced it had to be you!"

"And Sumit?" Sameer seemed resigned. "Why did you not consider him? Did you really not know how he felt about you?"

"Sumit and I have practically grown up together. We got into all kinds of trouble together and never once did he let me on to his feelings! He was the one who introduced me to Tarun as well. And he was the one who did go along with my planning, even though he was never convinced of them." I was stunned to even realise what this meant!! The fool that I was, I had been so blinded by this craze for Tarun that I never once realised what Sumit felt!!!!!!

"And now that you know how he feels, what do you want to do about it, Chanda? I always knew that what we have, however special, is not going to last. You still have your chance at making the right choice." With a tear to his eye and a constriction in his throat, Sameer said, "Make that choice, Chanda! Go to him. He has suffered a lot over the last few years."

Even before I could say anything, I felt a soothing breeze lift me up. "Wait!!! Sameer! I need to tell you something!"

"I am pregnant!" I screamed for him to hear me. He turned around one last time, and I thought that maybe, just maybe he heard me. But I had no way of knowing this.

Did I really choose Sumit over Sameer?? How could I have done that! Although I did not say anything out aloud, I must have chosen Sumit in my mind, because I was being carried away yet again into oblivion!!!!

CHAPTER 18

THE LOOP AGAIN

I was still trying to comprehend what just happened when I was swept away to another point in my life!!

I was on the damn college bus again!!

I had chosen Sumit!!! Was that also the wrong choice??? What did the Gods want from me??? Was I supposed to stay single for my entire life? I am sure Chandragupta ji would really enjoy this!

My thoughts turned to Sameer. And the baby that I was carrying!! Was I still pregnant? How the hell was I supposed to explain this to anyone! Horrified, I thought about my parents and the typical Punjabi conservative family that I had grown up in? What would everyone say?

All this while I had been focusing on myself, not even once questioning the fact that Sameer could also have been on the same spiral as me.

He had been here, The in-between for so much longer all because I was his choice.

This thought humbled me.

I hadn't known him long, but here I was, shedding a tear for him. Life it seems is unrelenting. It delivered blow after blow when you were least prepared. I had married Sameer and had settled in life. But yet again because of tarun, I was in this loop again. I mean this did start with us going for the inauguration of his and Seema's studio!!!

In a daze, I heard Sumit behind me, his voice endearing even now. He wanted to introduce me to his friends from college, which meant that I was about to meet Tarun. For the third time.

I had now realised that Tarun and I could not be. It was apparent to me that this was the start of my mistakes.

Maybe I was supposed to take it slow.

Maybe going out with him without telling my parents was what triggered this entire chain reaction.

Looking back at my future life, I did see that my father never did warm up to Tarun. I guess he never quite forgave him for trying to influence me into listening to him and somehow jeopardising my life. Although my parents never knew that I had planned on getting married to Tarun without telling them, somehow I am sure they had seen through me. Parents—you just cannot fool them!! They may turn a blind eye to a lot of things, but they know their children too well. And I had always been the one to cause mischief and have my own way.

Somehow I had to make it right with them as well.

"This is Tarun, my batchmate from College," said Sumit one more time.

Having come to yet another decision, I looked at Tarun, and then quickly looked away. I was not prepared to throw away this chance to make things work for me. Sumit seemed a bit perplexed by my reaction. "Are you okay, Moon? I have never seen you so quiet. Where are your giggles and snorts," he teased.

"Yeah, yeah, I'm okay. It's just that I missed you so much while you were away that it has now hit me that I will be able to catch up with you after almost a year," I replied, all this while hiding my face.

"So why aren't you looking at me?" he asked softly with a finger under my chin to lift my eyes to his. A tear slipped out of my eye, and I watched dumbfounded as he collected it onto his fingertip. This cannot be the way my story goes forward, I thought to myself. I now knew that he cared for me, but did he care enough to look out for me with a bun in the oven?? Can it be possible that this guy cared so much for me?

I shook the thought out of my mind, emotions too raw even now, and smiled up at him. "Jerk!!! Gotta girlfriend as yet, or all the girls rejected you already!!"

He looked away for a second and then turned back winking at me. "Naah, no girlfriend!! I am waiting for you."

With that, he simply walked away and chatted with the rest of the group.

I felt them, even before I saw them...the grey-green eyes looking at me and smiling, with a thumb pointing in Sumit's direction.

He was still looking out for me.

As I started to say something to him, he just simply disappeared.

CHAPTER 19

SUMIT

Sumit and I met in school. It was his first day I think when I noticed this rather shy boy sitting all by himself. I promptly went up to him and held out my hand. "Hi! I am Chanda and I am going to be your best friend." Little did we both realise what that friendship meant. We were together, with the same interests, laughing at the same jokes and even getting into trouble at times for disrupting classes.

Those days at school were fun. For all the crushes I had, Sumit had something or the other to say about them. And I never did like any of the girlfriends that he had. We had our fights as well. We fought like crazy, just short of killing each other. He would pull my hair tied neatly into plaits, and I would dig my nails into his arms to ward him off. He probably still had those marks.

And then, just like that school was over, he went to another city to study engineering.

And I was left here, with his memories which made me laugh more often than not. The times we spent together were full of childhood joys, of discussing the future, of boyfriends and girlfriends. He was the only one who was allowed to come over to my house. I grew up in a very conservative joint family, and so having friends over and that too boys, raised a lot of eyebrows!!

Soon I had to get off the bus. As I walked by, Sumit pulled my hair and whispered, "So what say, wanna be my girlfriend now, Moon, or still just a friend." His smile was teasing as he let go and I all but tumbled out of the bus, bewildered and speechless!!

CHAPTER 20

IS THIS LOVE?

As I got off the bus, I could sense myself being watched. I turned around and caught three sets of eyes boring down on me.

Tarun looked confused.

Sumit was smiling and so were his eyes, merry and full of life.

And then the grey-green signature of Sameer, which looked approving before they vanished once again.

What was this? What had I gotten myself into? A feeling much like euphoria was at the very tip of my heart. But suddenly I sobered up. I did not want to jump headlong into yet another situation, only to be scarred and then back to the Hell loop. I needed to be cautious. And I had the baby to think of.

The day after this confusing episode went by smoothly. College was fun and so I enjoyed all my classes on fabrics, sketching and stitching. I felt alive when I saw various bolts of fine silk and linen and excited that I got to work with them. My work reflected my mood that day. Some of my designs turned out great, lively and joyful to look at. But some just did not make sense, even to me after I had sketched them.

"What's up with you today, Chanda?" quipped Seema by my side. "So, you and Sumit? Are you a couple now," she asked me a question to which I had no retort. Were we heading in that direction already?

"Oh no!!!" I quickly replied. "That's just the way he has been ever since school."

"That's not true, Chanda, and you know it. This Sumit that we met today is far from the shy boy that we knew at school. He is a man now, and from the looks of it, has finally realised that he has been in love with you, like forever!"

"What are you even talking about, Seema?" I was even more confused now. I had never had romantic feelings for Sumit, and neither did he. But I wasn't so sure now. After having come back from the future yet again, I wasn't sure about anything actually. Hell, I knew him inside out, and with all the bumps and banters we had shared, not once had he ever said anything. We practically grew up together.

“You know, we placed bets on both of you in school,” Seema continued heedlessly. “We, as in our group from school, wanted both Sumit and you to hook up! You both look so good together,” she sighed dreamily.

“Did you know that he has been in love with you right from the time that he met you?” she questioned me. “He was so smitten by you that at times, he would be gazing at you when you weren't looking.”

This was news to me! I had never considered in my wildest dreams that Sumit could be more than my best friend to me.

Pushing aside these thoughts wasn't easy, now that the floodgates had been opened. I questioned myself over and over again, but not once did I find anything that could have suggested otherwise. He had always been there for me.

Hell, in my near future a lifetime ago, he was the one who had helped me get to Tarun?

Would he have done that if he were in love with me? Would he have sat with me innumerable times holding my hand, letting me draw strength from his presence?

A niggling thought slowly worked its way into my dumb brain.

Sumit always wanted my happiness above all. Even when I had decided to go ahead and marry Tarun, he asked me a million times if this is what I wanted. If I was sure of this! Was that his way of hinting that maybe I had other options as well?? His way of saying what he felt for me?? He had always been a man of few words.

I now knew without a doubt that I simply had to ask him. He would never take the lead. That's just the way he was.

It was the middle of the week and I did not know how to get word to Sumit to meet me. I was not expecting back home before the weekend, and going back in between the week would raise a lot of questions. And so I decided to take Tara, my sister, into confidence.

Tara is two years younger than me, and while I was finishing university, she had just joined.

Since her classes finished earlier than mine, she opted to stay at home with our parents as her travel time was also less.

The following day saw me waiting in front of her college gate.

“What's up, Sisi! What a pleasant surprise!!” Her hug and her smile took me by surprise because that last loop had been bad for both of us. She had been torn between me and the parents. And being the better of us, she stood by them. I had no idea what she thought about me. I had been thrown back into the cycle of hell, even before I could reconcile with my sister.

“I missed you so much,” I whispered as I hugged her with tears in my eyes. For her it was just a few days, for me it was an eternity!! And she had no idea of this.

“Hey, Sis! What's wrong?? I haven't seen you cry in a long time!” That just broke the dam that I was trying to hold upright!!

“Oh, Tara!! I have so much to tell you!! I am just so confused that I don't know what to do,” I wailed.

CHAPTER 21

THE REVELATION CONTINUES

"Come now, Chanda, don't make a scene here," admonished Tara. "Let's go to the canteen across the road," she all but pulled me by my arm.

I looked and felt like a mess in front of my little sister, who suddenly seemed to have wisened up right before my eyes, there and then. Gone was the mischievous twinkle she always had in her eyes. Instead, I saw deep concern, which made me cry even harder. I could not tell her about the fact that I had died and had come back to her, this time to correct my mistakes, or choices as the Gods had wisely said.

Tarun, Sumit, Sameer…in thinking about them all, I had hardly given a second thought to my sister who had been there all along with me. We had always been there for each other, defending and standing up for each other. Tara had gotten into fights to protect me right from our childhood. I used to be the timid one, while she was the tigress.

"Now tell me what's wrong," said Tara as soon as she had signalled the waiter for coffee and something to eat.

"I've been such a fool, Tara," I mumbled through a fresh bout of tears.

"There is this guy, who probably loves me like crazy, yet I never saw it. I've been with him ever since we were in school, and I never once saw beneath his smile and laughter. I mean what kind of a best friend am I if I don't know what he has in his heart? He's never said anything to me, but now, these last few days, I get strange looks from him that I cannot make sense of. He looks at me as if I am a priceless gift, as if I might break anytime, and he is there to protect me!" I was breathless as I finished my monotone with a sad smile.

"So, finally it has hit you that Sumit loves you!" exclaimed Tara joyously.

"About time, Sisi! He has been head over heels crazy for you for so long! It has been visible to everyone except for you!" she laughed and pulled me in for a hug.

"Wait!"

"What?"

"You knew…but how?" I was zapped and did not have the clarity of a single complete sentence. I was bewildered, yet could feel something building up inside me. What? I did not know as yet, a strange quiet calm began surrounding me.

"I've noticed how he looks at you when you are not looking. He cries when you are upset and tries to hide it from you. Everytime that you say bye to him when he has been over to our house, he cringes at the word, as if he is afraid to let you go. So many times over all these years, he just looks at you with a smile on his face, and the adoration all but pops out of his being!" Tara's words were like a news flash for me. Seema could have been mistaken, but Tara was too sharp to miss anything!

"You know, I once asked him outright about his feelings for you," she continued. "All in good time was all that he said."

"So, if he is making a move now, I'd say about time!" She flung herself at me and hugged me tight once again.

"It's now up to you sister dear, to see what you have deep down in your heart!! No one can do that for you. You need to think long and hard, evaluate your feelings, imagine what life could be like with him, or without." My little sister had matured in the few months that we had been apart, I realised and I had again been centred around I, Me, Myself...

"I need to meet him," I whispered. "Not at the moment, Chanda," Tara interrupted me. "First spend a few days thinking about it. You are now at an age where Mom and Dad are looking for a match for you. So you need to know what your heart feels, what it wants. Think hard Sisi, and let's talk when you come home over the weekend. Then maybe, you may want to talk to Sumit, before you talk to the parents," she winked as she drained her cup of coffee. "And now I have to run. Have a test in less than 15 minutes!!"

I sat there, lost in thoughts long after Tara had left. I had a lot of thinking to do and a lot to process. My mind was confused, with thoughts of Sumit popping up randomly. How he had once consoled me at school when I lost a dance competition, the way his eyes lit up when he laughed, the countless silly jokes that we shared. We were alike, two peas in a pod, yet we were different as well. While he was usually shy and quiet, I was the opposite, a chatterbox and a social butterfly. I thrived in good company, while he stayed on the sidelines, apparently watching me I now realised.

“Hey, Moon!” Fancy seeing you here!”

It was as if my mind had conjured him up! There stood Sumit, the familiar grin on his face and a light in his eyes.

I looked around, a bit terrified of I don't know what. What seemed like a few minutes had been two hours that I sat there by myself lost in thoughts. And now, the one person who had been occupying my mind for so long stood right in front of me. Uncanny!!! Almost as if I had willed him to me.

“Are you following me or what?” I tried to act my cheeky self and asked him with a smile. Try as I might, I could not hide my confusion behind the fake smile, and Sumit instantly caught on to it.

“What troubles you, fair Damsel in Distress,” he teased, although the concern in his voice was evident. ‘What has made you give up on humans and be surrounded by these cups of coffee? Won't do you any good if you don't talk it out of your system,” he added, looking pointedly at the empty cups on the table.

He sat down beside me and took my hand into his, a gesture so typical and familiar over the years, but now, they had a new meaning to them. I tensed immediately, and he pulled away with hurt in his eyes.

“Have I offended you in some way, Chanda?” he seemed a bit dejected. “I don't remember you ever pulling away from me, or closing yourself to me. What is it? You know you can tell me anything, right?”

The sadness and concern were too much for me to handle and I broke down yet again!! God, I looked like a mess I could tell, even without looking in a mirror. Here was the guy who supposedly loved me crazy, and I did not know what to do. I knew in my heart that he was more than just a friend, but would I ruin something if I rejected his love? Or would I eclipse a beautiful friendship by moving forward into unknown realms?

And I had to tell him everything about the loops as well. How could I not? And how could I explain my pregnancy to him, if he did not know about the rest?

I just had to. But first, I needed a few answers as well.

CHAPTER 22

THE BARING OF HIS SOUL.

"Since when, Sumit?" Mustering up all my strength, I looked into his eyes and whispered.

"How long have you loved me?"

"Since forever, my Moon," he whispered back, eyes bright with unshed tears, and a slight tremble in his voice.

"When you offered me your friendship, I think I fell in love without even realising it.

When you fought with me, I fell in love even more with you.

When you laughed at my silly jokes, I all but wanted to hold on to you forever.

And when you cried over lost competitions and ugly fights, I wanted to give you the world, just to see you smile again.

When I went away to college, I realised that the one person that I constantly missed and wanted by my side, was you.

When I get home, you are the one that draws me to you, even before I have greeted my family.

If this is love, then I have loved you forever, and now somehow life is not the same if you are not in it.

Spellbound and speechless! That is what I was, unable to do much as blink, lest this moment was to disappear forever.

For what seemed like an eternity, we kept gazing into each other's eyes, the world around us fading into oblivion. I saw my awe and wonder reflected on his face. I was in awe of the fact that this man, whom I had known for so long, had loved me endlessly despite all my flaws. He was accepting me as I am, loud, bossy, a bit selfish, and a lot talkative unlike him!!

For Sumit, I guessed he was in awe of the fact that he had finally been able to express his love for me! The one person that probably didn't know about his feelings was me, and now they were out in the open. A dam just burst and both of us were caught in the undercurrents.

"I love you, Chanda, with all that I have. I would like to marry you and make you happy for the rest of our lives," he whispered even as a tear rolled down my eye.

A flood of emotions now very clear to me unleashed themselves as I flung myself into his arms. I simply could not let go!

"Ditto!" I whispered cheekily into his ear, my eyes now shining with this newfound knowledge. I probably had loved him all along, but just did not know what it was. I had never imagined that my best friend could also be the love of my life.

"You have to say it, Moon", he grinned at me, "I have waited like, forever to hear that from you."

I don't think my words mattered to me, but for Sumit, they meant the world. "I…."

"I Mmmmm," I fumbled.

"I think I love you, Sumit," I whispered shyly.

"That's not enough, my Love," he slowly released my hand. "Thinking is not good. You need to be sure. I can wait till you are sure about your feelings. I want to be with you, but it has to be wholehearted! We have our entire lives ahead of us, and it has to be as beautiful as you."

"So take your time, think about it if you have to, and then come to me. I am not going anywhere, Love," he added as he stepped away.

Blowing a kiss at me, he walked out of the canteen. A sense of loss prevailed upon me, as I watched him go. What he said made sense. I had to be sure of these newfound emotions. The practical side of me tried raising its head, but my heart was not in sync with my mind it seemed.

Two days.

That was the time I gave myself to think hard. The weekend was approaching and I was going back home. Before I spoke to my parents as Tara had suggested, I had to be sure of my feelings. Was this love? Or just a rebound of what I knew was going to happen the minute I made a wrong choice yet again?

Strangely enough, the thought of going over and over again in the loop seemed undaunting, if only I could get to see Sumit again. I couldn't be on this Feris wheel for the rest of my life, could I? Practical me by my side whispered in my ear. "What life?" my heart shouted back!! I was already dead!! And this was a bonus. "Think about the baby," my practical side whispered again. That had me sober and thoughtful. And then the decision was made.

Yamraj Ji had said that we would not remember anything from our previous loops, and yet I did. And so had Sameer. That meant that I was still pregnant!! I will tell Sumit everything. I did not want to start a life with him without him knowing the truth of what had already transpired. I may be wicked, conniving and a person who would rather just run away from problems, but this man deserved to know the truth. And if this were to be my last chance at making things right, I would do anything to get it right.

CHAPTER 23

THE ACCEPTANCE

The day I got home, my home was in a flurry of activity yet again !! No! No! NO!

No way were my parents going to make me meet a candidate for marriage once again!

“Tara, what's going on,” I asked her frantically as I pulled her into our room. “Not a match-making session!!” I lashed out harshly.

“Oww Chanda!! Let go...you're hurting me,” Tara urgently whispered, as she pulled her arm away.

“And yes, we are going to meet a boy and his family for a prospective marriage alliance for you. You really must have been quite the rebel, that Mom and Dad want to get you married off so quickly!!” She laughed at the sombre expression on my face.

“Cheer up!! Maybe this will clarify your feelings and your mind as well. If after this meeting, you still feel that you don't love Sumit, then just get married to this guy."

"Says who!" I almost shouted back.

"Says who, Chanda? Use complete sentences, please. You are confusing me!"

"Says who that I don't love Sumit," I retorted back even before I could think.

"Ah, Ha!!" Tara exclaimed gleefully. "I knew it! Oh, I just knew it, I am so damn brilliant!"

Hugging me tight she said, "Don't worry Chanda! I am sure you will be surprised when I tell you who it is that has asked to meet you and your family!"

"Tara, your riddles are endless, and I love them. But right now I cannot think! This is all such a mess!! I need to tell the parents about Sumit!"

There was a sense of urgency in my manner which sobered up Tara. Even before I could contemplate my next step, Mom walked into the room, with a new suit in her hands.

"You don't need to dress up for this, Chanda, but all the same, please wear this suit. No jeans or dresses please! Whatever you want to say, say it after we get home darling," she smiled at me as I opened my mouth to speak. "We are short on time, and Dad does not want to get late! You know how he is a stickler about being on time," she rolled her eyes as she quickly walked away before I could get a word in.

With sparing me no time to think or to speak, my parents and sister quickly huddled me into the back of the car and we went zipping by to some restaurant to get this charade over with. I was seething with anger by now, since I felt trapped, but did not want to say anything until we got back home.

As I got out of the car, I spotted Sumit and his family!!! Great!!!!

Maybe he could convince my parents to let me make a choice. That was the first thought.

The second one jolted me into a panic mode, almost!

He was here with his parents. Maybe his folks were also forcing his hand to get married. We were almost the same age, me being about 10 months younger than him. The 90's was an era where if a girl crossed over to 25, she was considered too old for marriage. And I was 24!! So the actions of my parents were understandable.

But Sumit! He still had a few years before he was bound to marry. And what about the love that he had professed to me? I looked across at him and for once felt like tearing that grin off his face. What a jerk! When I had made up my mind and acknowledged my feelings for him, he is set to get married to the girl of his choice.

I was hurt. And for the first time that entire evening, I had nothing to say.

Since my parents had never met Sumit's parents and vice versa, it was Sumit who introduced them. I was perplexed when the waiter seated all of us at the same table. How on earth was I supposed to talk to somebody of my parent's choice while Sumit sat right next to me? Why was he even here and why was he looking at me constantly, as if willing me to look at him?

"Why won't you look at me, Moon?" he whispered. It seemed that somehow we had started conversing with each other in whispers now. Endearing as it was, at that moment I just wanted to lash out at him.

“Why are we here? I was forced by my parents to meet a prospective groom and his family. With you here, by my side, how the hell can I even look at anyone,” I muttered.

“Why?”

“Are you in love with someone, sweetheart?”

I wasn't used to such endearments from Sumit. So I simply nodded my head in the affirmative with wide-open eyes.

"And who may that be, I wonder,” although his tone had a light banter to it, I could see something flicker in his eyes as I gazed up at him.

“Do I have to say it right here, right now?”

“I am afraid so darling, Moon, only then can we move forward.”

“I love you, you Jerk!” I screamed out at him, not caring that we had an audience, for once not realising that my parents sat just a foot away from me.

Before Sumit could react, or I could add anything else, there was a whoop of joy from Tara on the other side of the table.

It was then that the fog lifted off my brain!!! Sumit was the boy that my parents had chosen for me!! And with Tara's help, they had set up this meeting!

“Miss Chanda Sabharwal, will you please marry me?” Sumit held out a ring in his palm and there was that silly grin on his face once again!!

Oh, my God! I realised I can never tire of looking at him for the rest of my life. He made me laugh, he cared for me, and he was always around and watching out for me. He loved me.

I wanted to shout out YES at that very moment, but something held me back. I needed to talk to him first and tell him everything. I did not want to deceive this man in front of me, who had in his own subtle way won my heart forever.

“We'll talk, My Moon. Pretty soon, but please say yes right now,” as usual he already knew what I was thinking. Without giving it another thought, I caved in.

“Yes!!!!”

No sooner had I uttered the word out of my mouth, I felt myself floating in the air. This is what euphoria felt like I thought.

And then it sank in!!! I made the correct choice!!!

CHAPTER 24

THE TRUTH

Once again I was in-between worlds. The world beneath me seemed to be calling out to me. I had only just fallen in love! Why did I have to be taken away so abruptly? The Gods could have shown me some mercy for having made the right choice. But who are we mere mortals to argue with them? What is bound to happen has to happen.

And so I floated onwards. My last and final chance at making things right. This time I found myself outside my lawyer's office!!

What! I thought to myself in disbelief! Did I screw up my life with Sumit as well?? Oh heck! What was wrong with me?

As soon as my feet touched the ground, it all came back to me. I was indeed married to Sumit, and yes, we had decided to separate!!!

My life with Sumit had been bliss! 28 years well spent in matrimonial harmony.

The day I said yes, was probably the happiest I had ever seen Sumit till then. But I also had a sword hanging over my neck. The pregnancy, and the baby!!!

Ever since my alleged time travels, I had no way of knowing how far into the pregnancy I was. I had to tell him soon. And then go see my gynac!!

A day after we said yes to each other, Sumit and I went on our first official date. It sounded a bit strange to me. I still had to get used to the idea that my best friend was soon to be my husband.

"Sumit, there are things that you need to know," I started shakily, as soon as we were at Nirulas, with a Hot Chocolate Fudge sitting between us. He never ordered one for himself, but would scoop out all the nuts from my ice cream!! The only one who got away with it.

"Alright, my darling Moon, shoot." I hated to be the one who could wipe that grin off his face. But this had to be done. I just could not bring myself to move forward without letting him into my past.

“Where do I begin?”

“From the very beginning, my love”.

“This may sound very weird and unreal to you Sumit, but please you have to believe me,” I started.

“This will not be the first time that I am getting married,” I stated pensively. “I was married to Sameer in the future.” This did not make sense to me, so how was it supposed to make any sense to Sumit, I cringed inwardly, trying to get across to him.

With a look of astonishment on his face, Sumit kept quite, waiting for me to continue.

“You see, I have come back from the future. I mean I have already lived my life up until 2020, when we shall be hit by the pandemic. I died in a freaking accident, and was sent back by Yamraj Ji to correct a few choices in my life. The first time I chose Tarun with your help, but things did not work out as I had planned. So I was sent back to make another choice. Or rather, correct my mistake.”

He still kept silent, intrigued yet patient until I had said it all.

'The second time that I came back, I chose Sameer. Tarun and Seema got together, and you all but shut me out of your life."

Still not a word.

"This is the third time that I have come back to this phase in my life, and finally with a lot of help and insight by what you said to me in the second loop, I have been given another chance. So far it seems right, cause I haven't been sent back to the loop still. So I guess you and I are meant to be. We are a part of each other and are supposed to be together."

There I had said what I had to. But I still had to tell him about being pregnant. Somehow that seemed the hardest part.

After what seemed like an eternity, where I was sure to be back in the loop again, he whispered, "It took you three lifetimes to realise what I have already known for the better part of my life." He smiled at me with his heart in his eyes and I was all but lost for words.

There was no parallel for how much this guy loved me! I was overwhelmed, my voice strangled with the tears in my throat and eyes.

“But that’s not all, Sumit”, I gulped. “I was pregnant when I was whisked away from the last loop.”

“I may still be pregnant with Sameer’s child.”

“The baby is a part of you as well, which in turn makes him/her a part of me automatically.”

I swear I could have just died and gone to Heaven right then! As yet I had no real feeling for the foetus I was carrying, but Sumit’s acceptance was a burden off my chest and finally I could refer to it as the Baby wholeheartedly.

“But what do I tell the parents?”

“Let’s worry about that when we arrive at that threshold,” he said, pulling me to his chest and then just holding me real tight.

I felt safe. I felt secure and very very much loved.

CHAPTER 25

MARRIAGE AND THE FIRST FEW YEARS

Sumit and I got married a week later in a simple affair. Exactly what we wanted. A court marriage with our parents and our closest relatives, followed by a grand reception. The dancing and merry making went on till the next morning.

We stayed with his parents in their house. I finally completed my degree in Fashion designing and Textile designing. Sumit was already interning for a firm in Noida and soon was offered a position in the same company in Mumbai.

And so began the next phase of our lives. We shifted to Mumbai about four months after we got married.

"You are like a breath of fresh air, each time I am near you, Moon." He still called me Moon playfully and I still called him Jerk lovingly.

The first thing we did when we shifted was look for a gynac. I was a bit worried because we were married four months and I was still not showing any signs of morning sickness, or a bulge in my womb.

“What makes you think you are pregnant, young lady?” The gynac asked me merrily.

I was speechless!!!

“But I have not been mensurating for the last two months,” I lied. It had been more than two months, and Sumit and I were sure that the baby was fine, since we took care of my diet and exercises etc.

“You may be under a bit of stress, or some deficiency,” she continued. “So let’s do a Blood profile and see what needs to be done.”

I walked out of the clinic dumbfounded, my emotions mirrored in Sumit’s eyes as well. I do admit that while I felt relieved, I was also a bit disappointed. I was looking forward to being a Mom!

Sumit seemed more sombre on the way back home.

"I am so sorry, Chanda! I can't even imagine what this means to you. I know how much you wanted this baby." He just held on to me consoling me. But I just looked him in the eye and let all my love flow through my body into his. "We have time, Jaan, we shall make many babies together. As beautiful as me, and as intelligent and kind as you." Finally he had the twinkle back in his eyes, as we walked away from the clinic hands entwined forever.

Nothing could go wrong now, I thought to myself, thanking the Gods up above for having been so kind to us.

It was a beautiful life that we built together in Mumbai. In our early days, we would be walking along Marine Drive endlessly. Dinner usually was Vada-Pao, which I simply loved and Pao-bhaji at Juhu.

Slowly and steadily, we bought a house for ourselves.

"Hey Jerk! How do you feel about being a father?" I asked Sumit three years into our marriage. I had just come back from the gynac and I was bursting to tell him! We were expecting!

"Did I manage to knock you up, Moon?" The twinkle in his eyes was unmistakable and my love for Sumit only just grew. I wanted to see him holding our child. Heck I wanted to shower him with all the love that I had.

The pregnancy was pretty much uneventful, except for the crazy cravings for apples that I had. And the late night runs to Bade Mia for Kebabs! Sumit did it all, right from rushing out to get anything that I felt like eating, to massaging my feet because I was so big, it hurt my feet.

Sharad arrived one rainy night in the month of June. Exactly as I had seen in so many Bollywood films. Dark, rainy night, difficult to navigate the rain, a labour that seemed endless while we drove to the hospital, a complication that resulted in a C-section, and lo and behold!

I woke up in the hospital under a haze of anaesthesia to see the most heart-warming moment that I could have wished for. My husband and my kid with their heads bent together, just gazing at each other.

I fell in love all over again!

Our parents took turns to visit us once we had Sharad home. I was back up on my feet in no time, not wanting to miss out even a second of my baby boy growing up. He would cry and my breasts would begin to overflow. "You are actually a cow right now,"' Sumit would joke much to the chagrin of his mother. She left no opportunity to scold him, if he so much as made fun of anything I said or did!! My mother-in-law turned out to be my greatest fan and my confidante in a lot of things.

No sooner had we settled into the normalcy of having a toddler on hand, I discovered that we were pregnant again!!!! Sharad was just over a year old, which meant that by the time he turned two, we would be six months pregnant!!

It seemed like an uphill task, but we were all game. "I want a girl this time," Sumit would whisper to me every night. "A girl it will be. I know for sure," I would reply back.

The pregnancy, like before, was pretty much uneventful. I was constantly on my feet since I had a kid to look after as well. Sumit helped as much as he could, but he was travelling quite a bit for work. His firm had a lot of projects overseas as well, which meant he would be trapesizing to Italy and France quite often.

September saw the arrival of Pooja, our daughter. And Sumit fell in love all over again! Pooja had my face from the start, my mom would say. “She looks exactly like you did, when you were born, Chanda.” “No No Bhabhi, Sumit was like this when he was born,” my mother-in-law would say. This was a friendly banter that would go on for the rest of our lives, I realised lovingly.

CHAPTER 26

THE NEXT DECADE

The next few years passed uneventfully. We were leading a comfortable life, the kids were growing up. My sister was married and settled in Australia. She had a successful interior decoration firm set up and in no time, was amongst the top notch designers in her field.

I was happy for her and applauded all the fame that she was getting. My work on the other hand was gradually picking up. I had managed to get a foothold in Bollywood finally and had a few films to my credit, where my designing expertise had shone.

Starting with a small fabrication unit at home, I had now a boutique to my credit and the young fledglings of film stars soon started visiting me. Things were looking good, and I was on the verge of being associated with big banners. My kids were growing up, my business was doing good, and Sumit was mostly absent.

Sumit was super busy as well. The year was now 2014 and finally Sumit was running his own design and consultancy firm. He designed bridges and from time to time would travel to sites to check on the progress of his designed bridges. This year, he was overtly busy with a project in Goa, which had been causing him sleepless nights.

"I understand Sumit, you are busy, but please Love, I have a very important meeting on the day that the children have their board exams. You have to make yourself available." I needed Sumit to be there for Pooja especially since she was writing her board exams for the first time. I probably was more nervous than her, but she was Papa's darling, and I just knew she relied on him more than she did on me.

Both Sharad and Pooja had to sit for board exams this year.

While Sharad was an ace student, he was more interested in being a chef. He had already selected a few universities abroad and was all set to excel in his chosen field. He planned to leave the country soon and had been working towards his goal for the last year and a half.

Pooja, on the other hand, turned out to be exactly like me. Fearless, authoritative and and imp! My mother's words haunted me each day…"I'll ask you when you have children of your own!" she would say whenever I defied her (which had been quite often, I now realised). She was great in studies when she put her mind to it! More often than not, Pooja could be found in front of an easel with paint smeared all over her clothes and face.

Pooja was set to be a painter, I could see. But nevertheless, she did have to sit for her examinations.Forever a dreamer, she had difficulty focusing on things that did not interest her, and school definitely did not interest her. I could only hope that she passed her 10th and 12th grade.

That's another story that she astounded us with her result each time!! She scored in the 90's percentile which made me heady and drunk with joy when her results were announced.

"Don't worry Chanda, I'll be there. You can attend your film thing with no worries."

"It's not A Thing', Sumit! It's one of the bigger banners asking for me to meet them with my designs. It's a period film!! I have to nail this somehow."

"It's the same thing," he shot back, with his familiar grin. God! He could be such a jerk with his comments and the next moment disarm me with his smile. I loved to hate him at times, I thought to myself, smiling at him with the love shining in my eyes.

CHAPTER 27

OUSTED FROM BOLLYWOOD

"What do you mean you cannot come for the meeting today Chanda?" You know that this is the final meeting for the costumes and the big shots are already here...waiting for you in fact!"

My friend, and my stepping stone into Bollywood Meher, was livid.

"Meher, listen Sumit is off to Goa. The bridge with his design collapsed!!! One person was killed and several others injured!. I couldn't ask him to not go! And I need to take the kids for their exams. I can only be there once I have dropped them back home in the afternoon." I tried clarifying my stance, but it did actually sound hollow to my ears as well.

A chance in a lifetime was slipping through my hands and I had no way of stopping it.

"They can go back home by themselves, Chanda!! You are needed here! The producers and the directors are not gonna wait for you forever…..and do you even realise how bad this looks on me?”

Meher was voicing my thoughts exactly, but I don’t know what took over me, as I blasted her about not understanding since she was not a parent as yet…

“Your call Chanda! I can only help you so much.” This statement sounded very final from Meher and I could sense her anger and frustration.

My missing work that day cost me my reputation and a friend!

Bollywood can be very unrelenting, I realised soon. I would be considered to design for a few small budget films, but soon enough the budgets would be cut down further and I was told that I couldn’t be a part of the film since it did not sit well in the budget!!!

It did not take me long to realise that my reputation preceded me everytime I was called for a meeting!

“Aren’t you the one who did not attend the meeting with Kanan Mohan?” “Weren’t you the one who lost out on ‘Don 5’?”

"Chanda Ji! You don't show up for meetings, how can we trust you, especially an outsider?"

I soon began to go into a cocoon, slowly and steadily. My work dwindled to almost nothing. Although it wasn't his fault, I was still angry with Sumit for not being there when I needed him the most. Months dragged on as I tried to fight depression. Sumit was hardly around. I needed him, but he was too busy sorting out his own mess.

CHAPTER 28

THE FINAL TURN

Things seemed to be going wrong at every turn. Even before Covid hit the world, my business had started to suffer. People no longer wanted Chinese goods. My textile designing firm had been importing a lot of cloth from China, where my designs were cheaper to produce. My designs, although popular, were being rejected because of being manufactured in China. This had an impact on the household as well. In today's day and age, a single-income family turns out to be very expensive to maintain.

Small quarrels about little things soon began turning into ugly fights and there was now a huge void between Sumit and me. Those early romantic days of marital bliss were replaced by sour faces and angry looks.

Things became unbearable when he drew up the papers and sold our house to pay our debts. I simply could not fathom this and walked out.

He had been trying to get me back home, but I was not ready to forgive him!!

I filed for divorce and I was coming out of the lawyer's office with the draft in my hand. We had a date with the judge a few days later.

As I stepped outside, I was blind to the sweep of the Marine Drive that I so loved.

Deep in thought, I guessed that the divorce was inevitable! We had been fighting like crazy these last couple of years! It was the year 2020, and the pandemic was a global thing now. It had robbed us of our routine, our business and our peace. Staying home for six months had affected both our businesses andwe were now on the brink of bankruptcy. I was home at the time trying to find manufacturers for my designs which seemed like an uphill task. Having to pay twice the price for a single bolt of fabric was running me dry.

Sumit had a lot of projects overseas in France and Spain. On the verge of being completed, his engineering projects now stood vacant. The kids were home from school and college and we were at our wit's end rationing daily needs just so that we could stretch our meagre savings.

That's when Sumit had decided to sell the house and move into a smaller place! His parents were long gone. God rest their souls, our daughter was all set to spread her wings, and our son was all set to go back to New Zealand as soon as the flights opened. He was working there and had left behind a girl he was all set to marry. So, we could have done with a smaller house.

What went wrong?

How did we end up here?

Do people like us, who had always been reasonable and practical and loved each other so much, still end up on opposite sides of a courtroom?

This could not be the end of us!

We could work things out I was sure, and what was even the harm in shifting to a smaller place. It seemed insignificant, considering the 28 years we had spent in bliss with each other.

I made my final choice.

With determination on my face and a very clear head, I called up Sumit.

"What is it now?" his gruff and rude voice on the other end almost broke my resolve.

"Hey, Jerk!" I tried keeping my voice steady, emotions too raw. "Wanna meet me for a decent coffee?"

"Where are you? I thought you were finally getting out of my life?" He was hurt, I could make out from his voice.

"I am at Marine Drive and I shall wait for you at our usual spot."

"Can we talk, please? As a team, as husband and wife," I pleaded with him.

"10 minutes, I shall be there." "And Moon," I could hear the pause in his breath, "I still love you, you know that, right?"

With a fresh zeal in me and a renewed energy to fight the world, I simply replied to him

"Ditto! Jerk!"

EPILOGUE

It had been two weeks since the accident!

I had finally made the right decision. The last one! I did not sign the divorce papers then.

As I had gotten into my car two weeks ago, I saw out of the corner of my eye, a man jogging. He wasn't looking where he was going and as I was about to accelerate, he stepped right into my path.

With a foot to the brake and a hand to the horn, I yelled out at him. “Hey!! Watch it.”

He raised his head and pierced me with the most unusual set of grey-green eyes. “I’m sorry!! I wasn't looking where I was going!”

“Are you okay? No sooner had the words left my mouth, I was jolted hard and my forehead hit the steering wheel! I was knocked unconscious.

A bus hit me from behind! I guess the accident was inevitable as well.

Somebody must have called an ambulance and Sumit, because the next thing I remember is being wheeled into a white sterile room. I was probably in and out of consciousness because I kept seeing Sumit, and then the eyes and then this huge black figure with the timid-looking man beside him.

Was I dead already?

No way! I played the game and won the last round. I had to be back with my family, my children and the man I loved and cherished—Sumit.

"All in good time, Chanda!"

I must have spoken up because the huge man in black was none other than Yamraj.

"I don't want to die Yamraj Ji," I whispered tearfully. "I only just started living again. I finally made the correct choices, and then you bring me here?"

"Relax, my child! You are going back to your family!"

I was getting my wish of getting back my family. This made me wonder. Will I be the same woman trying to make ends meet, waiting for her husband to get back home? Finishing her work quickly just so that she was home to prepare dinner for the family? Pick up after the kids, tend to the needs of her family.

But what about me?

What did I want out of life?

Did I really want to continue with my almost non-existing existence?

I had been writing again for the last few years and once or twice had been invited to women oriented events as a speaker. I was giving our idealistic choices and career tips to the younger generation now. But had I followed them through from myself?

My business had closed down even before the lockdown lifted. I had simply just given up. Ever since the Bollywood fiasco and then the pandemic, I had been writing fervently. It was a way of distracting myself from a now empty house and a marriage, which both of us were working on.

The past few years had been hell for Sumit and me. A lot had been said which could never be taken back. And a lot left unsaid. Both of us forgot to let each other know how much we still loved one another. But we stayed together leading completely different lives.

The accident had forced me to think about myself. I wanted more out of life. I had made a decision.

"Chitragupta, wipe the slate clean and send her back. She now knows what she wants." Yamaraj looked relieved, as if the weight of dealing with me had aged him twice or three times over!! The timid-looking Chitragupta smiled at me.

Even before I could comprehend what was happening, they were gone!

PRESENT DAY

THE JIGSAW IS COMPLETE.

The next time I woke up, I was at the gate of my college once more!!!!! But this time around, I was there to give a lecture on creative writing.

But I now knew what I wanted. I already knew what my choices would result into, and I was prepared.

One failed relationship, and two failed marriages later, with my children beside me and behind me I finally crossed over to the other side of the choices!!

I did not die!!

I just chose myself over everyone else. It became clear to me that love would never be enough for me. I could never be the typical wife or girlfriend.

Some people are not meant to be in a relationship. They desire much too many things, which sometimes cannot be found in one single human. I am one of them. I am just too strong an individual to let anyone overshadow me.

What took me a lifetime to see, my children saw as soon as they were old enough, and urged me onto the right direction. Right for me!

Sumit was there when I woke up from my accident the final time, holding my hand. All is well I thought to myself. I shall soon be able to go home. I looked at my best friend and whispered, "I love you."

He smiled and looked at me with unshed tears in his eyes, "Ditto, my Moon". I was discharged from hospital and Sumit drove me home.

"Wanna stay for a coffee?" I asked him half-heartedly, much too tired to actually make any.

Yes, you got that right. We did indeed stay separately now. It was a phase that we wanted to try, just so that both of us could breathe again. The unpleasantness had drained both of us and we needed time to unwind. So while I was in the hospital, we spoke together as friends. He needed space and I needed a change. The wounds inflicted by our words over the last few years were just too raw at the moment.

And so we were experimenting. I shifted into a condo nearby to regain my strength back. Both the kids were already getting on with their lives, so Sumit decided to stay with them while they were still home. Good for him, I thought to myself. He'd better make up for all the times that he was not there for them.

"Drop the act, Moon," he smiled." I'll let myself out, but you need to rest."

With that he left, and I was once again alone with my thoughts. The children were off to college and work and would be back after a while. I made myself a much needed ginger tea and settled myself to follow my passion—writing.

I was already commissioned to write my first book, after being an avid contributor to various magazines for the last few years now.

I quickly fired up my laptop, and opened a new Doc.

The name of the novel had been sitting with me and I penned it down without a blink or a second thought.

GOING BACK… FORWARD

9 789360 941840

Printed by Libri Plureos GmbH in Hamburg, Germany